Strategic Leadership

Foundational Frameworks for Effective Management

Josh Macalinao

Contents

Introduction

In an increasingly volatile and ambiguous business landscape, the need for strategic leadership has never been more acute. Leaders face a daunting task: to steer organizational strategy, align execution, and deliver results in complex environments filled with disruption. Those who can reliably convert corporate vision into reality represent the rarest of talents coveted across industries. What separates strategic leaders able to master uncertainties from those derailed by obstacles or distraction?

This book spotlights the underpinning mindsets, frameworks, and capabilities distinguishing the strategic leader's toolkit. It serves as an indispensable guide for both developing executives seeking to level up skills and seasoned veterans aiming to amplify impact. By highlighting research-backed insights paired with relatable stories demonstrating application, readers substantially strengthen abilities to:

- Construct mental models simplifying complexity

- Commit to clear priorities decisively

- Influence stakeholders through persuasive communication

- Structure dynamic execution rhythms that adapt

- Coach teams toward ownership and accountability

Many leaders instinctively recognize the need for such strategic talents but lack structured approaches to cultivate them. This book fills that gap as a comprehensive playbook for intentionally developing the cognitive, interpersonal, and executional toolkits vital for consistent leadership excellence. It equips readers with portable frameworks and micro-skills transferrable across diverse functions and organizations.

The opening section highlights crucial sense-making abilities allowing leaders to process complexity without getting overwhelmed. Chapter one explains techniques to structure strategic thinking using mental models as shorthand mechanisms to identify key dynamics within unfamiliar environments. Readers learn how leaders distill complex settings into simple situational frameworks so they can quickly size up priorities.

Chapter two delves into emotional regulation and impulse control as a seminal skillset enabling sound judgement amidst stressors like time pressure or interpersonal conflicts. Leaders discover tactics to short-circuit unproductive anxiety and frustration while summoning productive energy towards opportunity. This section concludes by spotlighting predictive foresight as a core leadership capability involving imagination, environmental scanning, and scenario planning. Readers will finish these chapters equipped with cognitive tools to reliably turn uncertainty into informed strategy.

With simplified understanding of complex contexts, leaders must next focus teams on what matters most. Section two opens by spotlighting skills for discovery-driven strategic planning starting with open questions rather than prepackaged solutions. Readers will grasp why building strategy is best conceived as facilitated dialogue rather than top-down mandates. Chapter five then addresses tools to align organizational attention on key priorities through techniques like OKRs for strategy setting and meeting rhythms establishing execution tempo.

Chapter six explains crucial project management methods allowing leaders to breakdown initiatives into governed workstreams tracking progress through defined milestones. Readers will grasp both waterfall and agile approaches while tailoring to context.

This section concludes with insights on financial acumen as an underappreciated leadership skill crucial for context amidst uncertainty. Readers will gain literacy around core financial statements and metrics to enable nuanced decision tradeoffs weighing risk, returns, and resources. Finance serves not just as a purely analytical domain but an invaluable leadership instrument for strategic communication and influencing stakeholders.

With priorities clarified, execution relies on effectively persuading and supporting talent. Section three opens by examining the science of persuasion, highlighting universal principles proven to motivate staff commitment. Chapter eight extends influence abilities by addressing tactical negotiation techniques useful when reconciling stakeholder differences. Leaders will grasp the interplay of interests and positions along with questions that empower compromise.

Section three concludes by spotlighting change leadership during times of deep organizational disruption. Readers will discover approaches for announcing, framing, and supporting structural transformation to both compel support and assuage uncertainty. Whether guiding reorganization, relocation, or strategic pivots, leaders require both inspiration and empathy when disrupting the known for the new.

The book concludes by spotlighting continuous improvement systems that embed adaptable learning organization-wide. Readers will understand how mature groups progress from reactive firefighting to continuous incremental optimization through deliberate frameworks like Lean. However, realizing such rhythms requires leaders first cultivating cultures embracing iterative development over fixed mindsets.

Leadership demands grow exponentially more complex by the year. Volatility stemming from socio-political upheaval, technology disruption, economic globalization, and market uncertainty show no signs of abating. Those helming modern organizations require nothing short of mastery over fluidity to keep stakeholders confidently aligned on value creation.

By spotlighting seminal tools and mindsets distinguishing strategic leaders, this playbook seeks to bolster clarity amidst ambiguity. It emphasizes universally applicable principles demonstrated through relatable stories of application across contexts from corporate titans to scrappy startups. Readers will finish these pages far better equipped to convert vision into collective victory regardless of role or industry.

Chapter One

Strategic Decision-Making

Decisions in business do not happen in a vacuum. As a leader, the choices you make are influenced by rational analysis, political dynamics, and emotional considerations. By understanding these forces and how they intersect, you can make decisions that effectively balance facts, relationships, and intuition.

At first glance, decision making may seem like a purely rational process of data analysis. In an ideal world, leaders would logically weigh pros and cons, run the numbers, and choose the best data-backed option. However, real-world decisions involve more than just hard facts. There is always a political dimension as well—you need buy-in from stakeholders who may disagree on priorities. And on top of all this lies emotional factors related to job security, public perception, and more.

So how can leaders make optimal decisions given these competing variables? The key is to address each facet systematically.

First, ground your choice in rational considerations.

Seek data, run scenarios, identify patterns from past experience, and leverage analytical tools to model potential outcomes. For example, a case study from Harvard Business Review revealed how the New Zealand Ministry of Social Development created simulation models to test the impact of various welfare reform policies, allowing them to quantifiably compare proposals. Fact-based analysis reduces uncertainty and provides justification for the decision.

Next, bring in stakeholders, listen to diverse opinions, and spotlight areas of agreement to uncover aspects most can endorse.

Research on group dynamics finds that participation in decision making and consensus processes increase organizational commitment. As highlighted in a Journal of Business Ethics study, leaders who actively integrate team input generate shared ownership over choices rather than unilateral mandates.

Finally, address emotional barriers by minimizing perceived individual risk.

Split decisions into modular components that limit any one person's exposure. Frame choices as collaborative ventures rather than isolated gambles. Set the tone by acknowledging self-doubt and emphasizing collective support. Studies of emotional intelligence and leadership emphasize that authenticity and transparency regarding fear or anxiety, paired with culture of psychological safety, promotes engagement over avoidance.

Balanced strategic decisions evaluate rational metrics, forge political coalitions, and mitigate emotional risk. With practice, leaders can blend analytical, social, and psychological competence to produce choices that optimize for essential performance indicators while ensuring stakeholder cohesion and personal readiness to execute. The result is end-to-end alignment driving successful implementation.

By deliberately analyzing data, building relationships, and validating emotions surrounding decisions, leaders can overcome common traps like groupthink that derail direction. Use the frameworks above to make decisions where facts, people, and feelings all point toward shared progress. And integrate lessons from past choices to hone intuitive pattern recognition over time, accelerating future strategic decision making through insight and experience. With dedication to rational, political, and emotional intelligence, leaders can guide their organizations forward with optimal outcomes prioritizing metrics and people alike.

The Role of Intuition vs. Analysis in Decision Making

As organizations become increasingly data-driven, decision makers often find themselves caught between the hard facts before them and their own gut feelings about the right path forward. With more information at their fingertips than ever before, leaders face rising pressure to leverage analytics in their choices. And yet, even the best data lacks the human context that intuition may provide. Navigating this tension requires recognizing the complementary power of analysis and instincts in decision making.

By deliberately combining evidence-based evaluation and experiential pattern recognition, leaders can reap the benefits of both rigorous quantification and quick qualitative judgments. The key lies in viewing them not as opposing forces, but as mutually reinforcing guides. Lean too far in one direction at the expense of the other, and decisions suffer from blind spots. Balance thoughtful processing of metrics with validation of emotional signals, and choices benefit from well-rounded input factoring in reason as well as reflex.

As strategies grow increasingly complex amid volatile, uncertain conditions, even the most data-savvy leaders cannot rely wholly on cold hard numbers. By activelylistening to and examining their own instincts alongside tangible analytics, decision makers gain an integrated perspective accounting for both conscious calculations and subconscious recognition of non-quantifiable risks and opportunities. The ultimate decisions thereby strike a nuanced balance between analytical and intuitive inputs for holistic evaluation.

Complement Data Analysis with Quick Intuitive Calls

In the digital era, leaders have access to more hard data than ever before, spanning both internal operational statistics and external market research. The advent of big data analytics introduces new depths of quantitative evidence to inform all aspects of strategic planning and decision making. And yet, counterintuitively, an overabundance of information can sometimes cloud judgments instead of clarifying them.

When facing seemingly endless datasets, analysis paralysis may set in. Business leaders can spend so much time gathering data, processing numbers, and debating metrics that forward progress stalls. Actionable decisions fail to materialize, or emerge too late to capitalize on fleeting windows of opportunity. In these scenarios, seasoned intuition derived from experience and expertise serves as an invaluable tool to cut through noise and catalyze movement.

As Harvard Business School professor Laura Huang's research on high-stakes decisions reveals, gut feelings inspire leaders to lean on their pattern recognition and make necessary calls amid uncertainty. Faced with urgent dilemmas like life-or-death surgery decisions or high-risk venture capital investments, intuitive reflexes provide the impetus to act quickly rather than endlessly debate data points. The gut thereby serves not as a replacement for careful analysis, but rather a complement accelerating its translation into decisive strategy.

Likewise, consider senior executives buried under data, as highlighted by psychologist Gerd Gigerenzer. When numbers fail to definitively dictate action, instinctive wisdom accumulated from past trials and errors steps in. Leaders draw on unconsciously embedded experience to respond rapidly based on global impressions. This tacit knowledge generates early hypotheses that focus subsequent data gathering to test reflective assumptions. Far from ignoring evidence, intuition guides its direction to maximize relevance.

In environments where competitive advantage hinges on real-time responsiveness, analysis alone moves too slowly while instinct isolated from facts invites reckless missteps. But together, the two enable both speed and insight. Leaders make choices faster by activating intuitive reflexes, then leverage data to validate the path forward. Blending instinctive conviction with empirical testing curtails second-guessing, empowering organizations to out-maneuver rivals.

Look Beyond the Numbers by Quantifying Intangibles

Confronted by qualitative concepts like company culture and employee satisfaction, many leaders hesitate to factor such intangible considerations into data-driven decisions. Unlike cut-and-dry metrics like costs, clicks, and conversions, these socioemotional components elude simple quantification and therefore get dismissed as irrelevant to analytical processes. However, leaders who deliberately mine fuzzier datasets for insights counterintuitively make better decisions precisely because they incorporate human realities beyond spreadsheets.

Recall how Google's Project Oxygen compared qualitative feedback from over 10,000 employee performance reviews to retention rates, identifying key management behaviors that boosted team morale. They then implemented leadership training programs that rapidly improved favorability scores. Despite the challenge of codifying soft skills into measurable analytics, Google's comprehensive approach yielded superior results by accounting for both emotional and empirical variables.

Moreover, while personal familiarity with proprietary data streams can breed false confidence, comparing numbers against industry benchmarks and academic research introduces constructive objectivity. Leaders who reference external contexts avoid insular mindsets and spot correlations that may otherwise go unnoticed. An advertising executive managing a campaign, for example, can gauge effectiveness more accurately by cross-checking their metrics against competitors and macro trends instead of evaluating performance in isolation.

In essence, effective leaders seek data behind all variables influencing business outcomes, whether qualitative or quantitative. They dismiss neither form of insight, judiciously quantifying each through triangulation. This holistic analytics integration provides the most complete operational picture upon which to base decisions aligned with both human and financial realities. By patiently extracting observations from soft data that reflects culture and relationships, leaders arrive at choices substantiated by well-rounded evidence.

Resolve Conflicts through Curiosity, Not Snap Judgements

Nearly all leaders eventually encounter dilemmas where data points toward one solution while instincts suggest an alternate path. Traditionally, this tension triggers frustration as decision makers feel pressured to immediately suppress discomfort and force resolution. However, thoughtful leaders can improve choices by instead cultivating curiosity about contradictory inputs.

By taking time to examine both factual evidence and countervailing emotions, leaders glean pivotal context. The data may appear sound on its surface yet still omit subtle risks discerned unconsciously. Alternately, intuitive hesitation could signify entrenched biases that the hard numbers debunk. In either scenario, curiosity uncovers essential observations that flip simplistic binaries to nuanced synthesis.

Productively navigating this tension begins with metacognition to name, then analyze, conflicting feelings. As author Cheryl Strauss Einhorn suggests, rather than ignoring or effortfully repressing uncertainty because emotions seemingly undermine rationality, lean into contradictory instincts:

- "The data looks good, but I'm feeling anxious and fearful. Could my gut be sensing a potential risk that the numbers aren't showing?"

- "The data is telling me something I didn't think it would, and I'm feeling frustrated. Might I be resistant to let go of my original hypothesis?"

- "Now that the data is in, I'm feeling a sense of discomfort. Could there be a reason to distrust the data? Or could I be realizing that this decision is rooted in a bigger issue than I first thought?"

This self-reflective move to label and inspect emotions creates psychological distance that prevents knee-jerk reactions. Leaders thereby avoid snap dismissals of either data or intuition. Instead, they explore the space between, uncovering invisible variables that escape one-dimensional focus on just facts or feelings. The result is decisions enlightened by interwoven analytical and instinctive integrity.

Superior strategic decisions do not blindly follow data points nor ignore analytics for impulse and intuition. By consciously counterbalancing empirical evidence with experiential pattern recognition, leaders amplify the strengths of both while mitigating inherent limitations. Quantifiable metrics coupled with qualitative human judgments increases choice resilience for long-term success amid volatility. Savvy decision makers thereby persistently refine and reinforce dynamic equilibrium between data-driven diligence and instinct-fueled agility.

Frameworks for Effective Decision-Making

As a leader, every choice you make carries consequences for your organization and team. In complex, ambiguous environments, determining the best path forward is far from straightforward. There is no singular formula that guarantees perfect decisions, but leaders can improve processes and outcomes by adopting a deliberate decision-making framework. When critical moments arise, a well-honed structure for analyzing options and choosing the right course guides better judgement even amid uncertainty. Equip yourself for difficult calls by following the steps below.

Step 1: Evaluate Possible Solutions Before Selecting One

The first phase of strategic decision-making sets the stage for final selection through expansive exploration of possibilities. Start by brainstorming ideas across various alternatives instead of defaulting to traditional responses or assumptions. Related research on creative problem solving highlights the power of divergent thinking before convergent choices. Expand your options before evaluating them.

To generate ideas independently or collaboratively, leverage proven techniques like design thinking workshops, SWOT analysis of internal strengths versus external opportunities, lean startup "pretotyping" experiments, and devil's advocate debates. Look beyond the obvious to uncover fresh insight from new voices and peripheral perspectives less wedded to existing conventions. Diverge broadly before converging narrowly. Document all potential solutions without immediate critique so you can comprehensively compare later once full context emerges.

Even once leading proposals surface, continue listing backup plans. Schedule time post-decision to revisit runner-up concepts in case implementation reveals flaws in the selected direction mid-course. Avoid wedging on a single possibility or determining one perfect answer too soon. Sustained curiosity, flexibility and scenario planning equip leaders to pivot amid volatility.

Step 2: Define Responsibilities and Timelines Before Committing

With an expansive set of options documented for consideration, next clarify procedural logistics to inform evaluation. Determine decision timeframes, delineate duties, confirm authority and specify accountability structures preceding final commitments. Actively answer:

- Who owns ultimate choice? Is responsibility individual or shared?

- What deadlines or external dependencies apply?

- Who governs approvals? What sign-offs are needed?

- If selected course fails, who manages consequences?

Solidifying these dynamics early enables smoother downstream assessment as key players know their roles. It also surfaces potential disconnects around permissions and ownership to reconcile differences through open dialogue, not last-minute tension. Establish collective understanding around resource constraints, reporting lines and risk exposure front-end so that final decisions adhere to agreed bounds.

Moreover, decide how much calendar time this evaluation warrants based on tradeoffs around depth versus speed. Complex calls with companywide impact justify extensive diligence over quick response for example, while time-sensitive scenarios warrant efficiency. Align decision velocity and rigor to context. Set targets for both idea generation and final selection to prevent open-ended delays.

Step 3: Gather Holistic Input to Illuminate Blind Spots

Before assessing options, dedicate effort toward compiling complete, balanced information from varied lenses to enlighten evaluation. Since decisions suffer from biased, limited inputs, proactively seek facts that challenge assumptions and broaden perspective.

Gather diverse data by distributing research across specialized domains and vantage points. If tackling a market expansion decision for instance, assign leaders to quantify costs, forecast demand, evaluate competitors and survey customer sentiment. Reconvene findings to synthesize insights from these distinct dimensions into an integrated profile identifying subtle correlations.

Likewise, pull benchmarking metrics from past decisions alongside present proposals to detect deviations from norms. Reference industry standards outside internal environments prone to normalized groupthink. Input expansiveness reduces insularity, exposing blind spots. Position choices on spectrum of evidence, not gut reactions, through exhaustive reality-testing.

Of course, leaders balance data gathering with analysis paralysis avoidance. Perfect information remains elusive. Given more data always exists, determine "enough" based on risk tolerance and outcomes at stake. Then forge ahead with sufficient intelligence for reasoned evaluation, even if uncertainty lingers.

Step 4: Weigh Risks and Rewards When Assessing Alternatives

With foundational parameters and initial research complete, conduct robust feasibility analysis of options themselves. Compare potential solutions against values-aligned priorities discussed below to determine suitability. Think through implementation pathways anticipating challenges that could derail ideas in reality. Pressure test proposals through "pre-mortem" consideration before commitments.

Additionally, leaders explicitly quantify upside opportunity versus downside risk for each path under consideration. Calculate worst case scenarios, but also best case payoffs. Assess both extremes' plausibility given available data. Gauge expected ratios between reward and hazard tailored to situational risk appetite.

In some contexts, playing it safe makes sense despite modest returns. But in transformative moments, responsible risk-taking fuels breakthroughs through purposeful innovation. Consider both probabilities and outcomes when evaluating risk-related tradeoffs. Recognize even carefully vetted proposals carry uncertainty. Then determine which option aligns to risk sensitivities given external landscape factors and internal capabilities. Weigh upsideagainst downside across alternatives accordingly.

Step 5: Let Values and Ethics Shape Your Perspective

Since all complex decisions involve nuanced tradeoffs with grey areas, leaders require core values and ethical compasses to guide choices absent definitive right answers. When confronting ambiguous choices rife with paradox, individual and institutional values serve as tiebreakers between equally logical options. Define and revisit these grounding beliefs throughout assessment.

Start by privately clarifying personal values driving your leadership purpose. What issues do you care about most deeply? What principles guide your choices in difficult situations? Then broaden conversations to surface organizational values and mission. Where do institutional identities intersect and diverge from individual ones? Discussion both aligns teams to shared goals and reveals conflicting assumptions requiring reconciliation through constructive debate.

Keep these central value statements handy as reference checks shaping option evaluations. When logics conflict, values tip balances by providing moral orientation to complex dynamics where technical data alone fails. They act as decision-making litmus tests revealing which options best align priorities with behaviors despite uncertainty. Allow both individual conscience and collective cultural wisdom to inform calls.

Step 6: Chart Tradeoffs Between Pros, Cons and Unintended Consequences

With risk profiles defined and potential pitfalls explored, catalog concrete pros and cons associated with each solution set. Moving beyond theoretical analysis into applied assessments sharpens viable distinctions. Comprehensively map advantages and disadvantages for accountable comparison.

Consider build cost estimates, rollout timelines, talent requirements, opportunity ownership structures and capability sustainability. Factor both immediate and second order effects. Delineate direct benefits and obvious downsides together with subtle unintended consequences that may emerge over time. Question assumptions driving projections through repeated inquiry from diverse viewpoints. Implications often cascade so scrutinize systemic interconnections, not isolated variables.

As patterns surface revealing options' asymmetric impacts on priorities, determine which tradeoffs leadership accepts versus rejects based on risk parameters and value alignments. Eliminate choices whose cons outweigh potential pros within situational contexts. Recognize remaining solutions all carry imperfections requiring navigation. Prepare contingency plans for likely implementation obstacles associated with each viable pathway.

Then finalize selection by revisiting foundational parameters around decision rights, accountability, resourcing and speed. Reconfirm chosen direction adheres to key bounds and addresses original catalyst dilemma. Maintain flexibility for redirection if environmental shifts warrant. Right-size conviction levels to magnitude of unknowns.

Step 7: Implement with Decisiveness While Retaining Openness

With above steps thoroughly completed, leaders ultimately forge ahead decisively upon final choice, executing with confident commitment while retaining adaptability should conditions change. Communicate the why behind decisions transparently to enroll stakeholders in driving successful adoption. Model personally the behaviors desired from teams and colleagues to motivate belief.

At the same time, acknowledge uncertainties inherent in even optimal complex decisions. Monitor progress indicators flagged during evaluation to enable real-time course correction if original plans prove flawed. Quickly re-engage key leaders behind pivots to reestablish ownership and prevent inertia. Frame redirections through lens of learning and growth, not personal shortcoming.

Finally, revisit archived runner-up solutions later to harvest backup ideas or resurface dormant concepts for fresh reception across distance in time. Refer back to decision journals to improve future choice clarity by learning continuously from reflection on past resolution processes.

Decision-Making Under Pressure

As a leader, you will inevitably face high-stakes decisions without the luxury of extensive analysis. When critical moments arrive demanding immediate response, anxiety understandably arises. In these pressure-cooker scenarios, how can you rapidly weigh alternatives and confidently move forward? Rather than freeze or act rashly, rely on the time-tested techniques below to sharpen focus, tap intuition, and steer your team through uncertainty.

The First Step: Manage Your Own Mindset

When tensions spike, instinct tells us to either fret endlessly about downside risks or impetuously speed toward initial gut reactions. Both responses tend to cloud sound judgement. So when confronting pressing dilemmas, leaders must first self-regulate thought patterns.

Anxiety thrives on hypothetical disaster projections that distract more than protect. Doubt yourself less and doubt the problem more. If you fixate on failing, you likely will. Direct attention instead onto navigating dilemmas. Define succinct success parameters before assessing barriers. This solutions focus calms nerves while catalyzing progress.

Likewise, some decisions require political sensitivities beyond personal reflexes. Impulsive choices satisfying in-the-moment urges often overlook interpersonal ripples. So regulate rash instincts with patience. Slow down to understand stakeholders, complications and motives before reacting. Responsible leaders discern when to trust their gut or test assumptions first.

In essence, operating under pressure demands managing your mental state above all else. Clear overthinking and underthinking by focusing deliberately on most vital factors set against desired outcomes. Project confidence to limit hesitation. With presence and purpose established, sound decisions follow.

Construct Scenarios and Responses in Advance

Of course, regulating mindsets in the heat of high-stakes moments proves extremely difficult without preparation. Top performers therefore invest heavily in scenario planning before crises hit. Mentally rehearsing a range of futures equips leaders with rapid response capability when situations inevitably arise.

Start by brainstorming across hypothetical dilemmas, potential points of failure and worst case disasters related to your responsibilities. Conduct "pre-mortem" analysis detailing imaginable threats. Specify triggering conditions, second order effects and resulting decisions for each. Catalog options with pros and cons to create quick-reference crisis playbooks should scenarios materialize.

Also liaise with trusted advisors to pressure test your logic across assessments. Discuss possible situations and proposed responses. Refine plans through alternative vantage points guarding against insular bias. Develop collective understanding of individual contributions within response frameworks should contingencies require mobilization.

By war-gaming outcomes, leaders gain double benefit of reducing risk through early mitigation while priming decisions for velocious execution when pressed into action. Stay vigilant for blind spots but expect the best. Mentally equipping for turbulence keeps teams grounded enough to smoothly navigate. Rehearse often so responses flow naturally.

Hone Your Ability to Appraise Context Quickly

When volatile events thrust leaders into consequential spotlights, rapid appraisal of priorities separates those ready for primetime versus those caught flat-footed. Attune skills to swiftly size up situational specifics, discard distractors and identify vital few inputs upon which choices turn when pressure mounts.

Start by consciously avoiding snap judgements tied more to emotions than empirical observations. Neutralize bias by pausing to breathe before reacting. Regain balance and distance to see clearly before proceeding. Ask clarifying questions to confirm or correct initial assumptions against reality. Maintain receptive dignity in chaos.

Then triage information flows for relevance using activation energy estimates. Which inputs offer greatest influence on desired outcomes if addressed? Categorize new data as either immediately actionable or less timely to file away. Funnel focus toward most timely and consequential factor convergence to keep momentum.

Leaders capable of urgent discernment operate decisively amid uncertainty since they reliably grasp contexts quickly at critical junctures. They neither tolerate paralysis by analysis nor fall victim to underinformed errors. They prepare, listen and steer discussion toward central issues confidently. Practice separating signals from distracting noise during calm to determine what truly matters when facing firestorms.

Trust Your Intuition but Verify Its Validity

Intuition powers our best rapid judgements, but only when grounded in expertise. If longtime experience has encoded recognizable patterns into your subconscious, then go with your gut intuition as an accelerant. But first verify foundational conditions match previous contexts. What feels familiar here and now versus distinctly new? Question unearned confidence by qualifying relevance before proceeding on just a hunch alone.

Use intuition as an entry point to further investigation, not ending point avoiding deeper diligence. Consider emotional pulls as hypotheses to examine, not absolute conclusions. Check for consistency against past decisions and key metrics. Investigate further using inputs from diverse lenses before committing solely based on instincts.

Distinguish qualified intuition derived from earned pattern mastery versus unqualified impulses reflecting bias or misplaced assumptions. Those lacking extensive direct background lean more heavily on data gathering versus reflexive reactions. But even veterans avoid complacency by deliberately revisiting guided assumptions as extra due diligence insurance. Blend intuition and analysis customized to situation.

Decide Confidently but Communicate Conditionally

Ultimately when authority requires decisive action amid complexity, leaders must choose pathways absent consensus from competing options rife with tradeoffs. After vigorously vetting scenarios, weigh alternatives against core priorities to formalize commitment toward one aligned vision. Then move boldly according to plan while remaining receptive to new inputs warranting course correction.

When broadcasting decisions outwardly, frame resolutions in direct language conveying certainty while acknowledging potential need for later adaptation. Eschew ambiguous messaging but remain intellectually humble. Explain current rationales completely while inviting questions to sustain buy-in should future pivots require stakeholder partnership. Model self-assuredness blended with humility.

No choice seems right when made yet history judges leaders on outcomes alone. But by incentivizing teams toward shared ownership, you distribute both risks and rewards. Position decisions as progress platforms, not permanent solutions. Adopting this growth mindset sustains team resilience to course correct cooperatively if new pressures later arise. Confidently commit then remain loosely tethered to enable agility.

During extreme uncertainty when immediate response holds serious consequence, decision delay risks compounding issues through inaction as problems worsen. But decision speed absent structured process risks reactionary errors or overlooked complexity derailing direction. Navigating this tension separates sound leaders from short-lived ones when pressure strikes. Rely on the above advice to sharpen judgement and unite teams when facing crucible moments in the spotlight.

Key Takeaways and Final Thoughts on Strategic Decision-Making

Key Takeaways:

- Manage your mindset first when facing high-stakes decisions under tight timelines. Redirect focus away from worrying and toward solutions-oriented analysis.

- Proactively scenario plan by envisioning potential crises and responses before urgent pressure hits. Mentally rehearse a range of options.

- Hone skills to swiftly size up situational priorities amid chaos. Rapidly identify the vital few factors upon which the decision outcome relies.

- Leverage qualified intuition tied to extensive expertise while still verifying assumptions. Question emotional pulls lacking empirical support.

- Decide firmly on direction then communicate conditionally on adjustments if new inputs emerge. Model confident humility.

Performing Under Pressure: Cultivating Agile Decisive Capabilities

Pressure reveals character. As external complexities compound and pace accelerates, a leader's ability to act decisively amid ambiguity separates high performers from the rest. When crucial choices carry consequence, reluctance risks lost momentum while reckless impulse invites disaster. Navigating tensions between paralysis and precipitation requires resilient thinkers able to hold steady convictions lightly with flexibility to update understandings. By deliberately developing supple cognitive capacities, leaders position themselves to respond reliably when pressed into high-stakes action.

Constructing Playbooks for the Fog of Uncertainty

Volatility abhors predictability but humans crave assurance. Navigating this paradox mandates envisioning multiple futures while securing present priorities. Mentally rehearse crises before their debut then target strengths against downside risks once turbulence hits. Confidently commit to direction without clinging to plans rendered obsolete by new realities. And rally stakeholders through fluid frames that say "we stand firmly here...for now open to where new light leads next." Great leaders thereby lift teams toward hope on horizons beyond fear.

The Mindset Divide Between Winners and Losers

When pressure mounts, average leaders simply react while proactive ones respond according to prepared principles. Where one spirals, the other rallies their best. How? By conditioning mindsets to default beyond doubt into discerning initiative. They resist inertia by remaining centered enough for one bold stroke instead of aimlessly thrashing. And they invest deeply in people by extending trust that ignites talent. Thereby earning solidarity sufficient to turn tanks quickly when threats encroach. But none of this manifests under fire if not firmly rooted through habits over time. So daily rehearsals render complex simple through venues high and low. Making leadership under pressure more dance than dogfight. The question then becomes not "are you ready" but "how soon can you get here." Because this place was built for you. But the door only opens from the inside out.

So now we stand at the frontier with future promising nothing and everything at once. How will you lead? The map you need reveals itself in trusted teams ready to care for gains won and lessons earned. Command yourself and serve others by example. Then watch followership flourish. And know that pressure is merely the price for influence worth its provocation.

Chapter Two

Embracing Uncertainty in Leadership

We live in an increasingly volatile and ambiguous world. As leaders, the decisions we make have wide-ranging impacts on our organizations and stakeholders. Yet how can we make sound choices when faced with unfamiliar terrain or limited information? By embracing uncertainty as the new normal.

The Myth of Prediction

It's only human to believe we can foresee probable scenarios and prepare accordingly. But reality often defies even our best projections. As the pandemic demonstrated, both optimistic and pessimistic assumptions tend to underestimate the extremes. Supply chains shattered while virtual connections thrived, underscoring the unpredictability inherent in complex, interconnected systems.

Rather than seeking impossible prescience, we must accept uncertainty as intrinsic to leadership. Scenario planning can widen our perspective on possibilities without blinding us to surprises. Tracking leading indicators helps detect emerging changes without relying on fortune-telling. And maintaining robust strategies with inbuilt flexibility allows quick pivots when circumstances shift. Leaning into uncertainty opens more creative pathways forward.

The Trap of Overcomplication

When facing multifaceted dilemmas, we often defer decisions while gathering more inputs and analytics. But excessive delays can paralyze progress at the cost of missed windows. How can leaders determine when they have "enough" information?

First, parse the problem into its constituent parts. Eliminate any extraneous components unrelated to the core issue. Next, take stock of which facets contain critical unknowns versus areas where you can extrapolate or speculate reasonably. Get clear on which insights can be obtained quickly and which require longer-term research. With this landscape mapped, you can then weigh the risks and benefits of potential choices given current knowledge.

There may still be gaps, but resist waiting for complete certainty. Set a deadline aligned with business needs, stakeholder expectations, and market dynamics. Trust that taking decisive action with 70% confidence today is better than over-analyzing at the cost of missed opportunities tomorrow. Of course, be ready to course-correct as fresh data emerges post-decision.

The Outcome Bias Trap

When assessing past choices, many default to judging quality by eventual results rather than logic applied. But this outcome bias obscures our ability to extract learnings. Positive ends may mask poor decision-making while negative impacts don't inherently signal errors.

To avoid this trap, establish processes that distinguish decision analysis from outcome analysis. Conduct pre and post-mortems on judgments divorced from their consequences. Track the soundness of logic, use of evidence, risk mitigation tactics, and stakeholder alignment independent of what ultimately occurred. Doing so provides a more accurate picture of what works and what requires recalibration. It also encourages bolder experimentation knowing that failure won't be penalized as long as rigorous reasoning is demonstrated.

Of course, uncertainty will persist as the norm, not the exception. But by embracing unpredictability, avoiding paralysis, and evaluating decisions on their merits, leaders can traverse ambiguity with savvy, agility, and purpose. The path forward may not always be clear, but with principles to guide the way, have confidence that strategic next steps will illuminate themselves.

Making Decisions in Uncertainty

Our fast-changing, intricately networked world overwhelms linear logic and confounds even the most rigorous forecasting models. As tempting as it may be, we can rarely amass enough information to guarantee "right" answers. Despite exhaustive research, unexpected developments outside our control inevitably materialize. And yet an apparent desire for certainty locks many leaders into denial, paralyzing progress across sectors and industries worldwide.

Leadership demands weighing options and charting direction in the face of incomplete information and unpredictable variables. Though we may wish for definitive data sets and formulaic solutions, the reality of management forces us to act amidst uncertainty. Rather than a weakness or failure, ambiguity is the default backdrop for executives and entrepreneurs alike. By acknowledging this inescapable truth and deploying strategies tailored for opaque conditions, we can traverse the fog with newly emboldened vision.

By accepting ambiguity as intrinsic to leadership, we liberate ourselves from false hopes of minimal risk and perfect outcomes. With this more accurate paradigm in place, we open capacity to navigate opacity with flexibility and creativity instead of anxiety or blame. The fog may persist, but our footing grows surer in its midst. Scenario planning, tracking leading indicators, and building adaptable systems provide tools to traverse the haze without pretending it can disappear entirely. The first step, however, requires acknowledging that the terrain ahead will remain imperfectly visible.

Strategies for Navigating Uncertainty

Once leaders embrace ambiguity as ever-present, what practical steps can guide decision-making amidst suboptimal conditions? Five key tactics help transform uncertainty from an obstacle into a catalyst for progress.

1. *Seek diverse perspectives* - Rather than relying solely on past precedent, open up your process to multiple inputs through debate and dissent. Mitigate individual biases by involving a range of stakeholders in framing issues and evaluating options. Facilitate an environment where all contributors feel psychologically safe to question assumptions and introduce alternate hypotheses. The collective wisdom generated sparks new possibilities while exposing blind spots.

2. *Structure decisions experiments* - When precedent provides limited guidance, run small tests to generate new data. Set decision criteria and metrics for success. For example, a bank uncertain which queue layout best serves customers can try three formats across different branches, tracking variables like wait times and satisfaction. These rapid experiments build knowledge while containing risk, informing iteration toward optimized solutions.

3. *Expect imperfection* - Even rigorously researched choices may disappoint half the time. But process matters more than outcomes alone. By grading decisions on sound logic rather than just results, we extract valuable learnings for future improvement. Moreover, with margin for error built in, occasional failures become acceptable provided the reasoning proves defensible. Room for imperfection thereby encourages bold experimentation and advancement.

4. *Focus on process alignment* - Since ambiguity clouds universal truth, ensure chosen paths resonate with organizational values and priorities. When data cannot dictate direction, north stars like vision statements clarify appropriate responses amidst uncertainty. If empowering customers represents a core belief, resolving a complex complaint to nurture trust may take precedence over short-term profits. Internal cohesion provides guide rails when external signals grow faint.

5. *Communicate courageously* - Transparency regarding information gaps quells unrealistic expectations while rallying stakeholders to collaborate. Highlight where conjecture filled holes and acknowledge surround ambiguity. Directly confronting uncertainty breeds camaraderie to address endemic challenges creatively. Silence, conversely, breeds anxiety and mistrust. Opening dialogue around navigating the unknown with imperfect inputs demonstrates confident leadership.

Rather than vainly seeking to eliminate uncertainty, leaders must anchor themselves amidst the turbulence by adopting new mindsets and tactics. No magic solution unveils a clear path forward, but principles like embracing collective wisdom, experimenting iteratively, and aligning to internal purpose can illuminate enough stable terrain for progress. Perpetual ambiguity may force us to proceed tentatively, but by walking in step with courage and transparency, entire organizations can traverse the haze - and even thrive within it. The route remains imperfect, but the journey continues.

Risk and Uncertainty

From pandemics to technological disruption, modern business resembles a stormy sea filled with rogue waves and unexpected squalls. Leaders must chart direction amidst this turbulence, guiding stakeholders towards safe harbors or even serendipitous discoveries.

But doing so requires both accepting perpetual uncertainty and deploying strategies to counterbalance associated risks.

Instability and doubt define today's rapid-fire marketplace, demanding nimble responses to sudden shifts. Technological innovation accelerates at exponential pace while consumer preferences grow more fragmented by the hour. Entire industries transform practically overnight, leaving once-dominant brands scrambling to adapt or facing abrupt extinction.

By definition, uncertainty introduces variables impossible to predict with any reliability, increasing the likelihood of suboptimal or even disastrous outcomes. When the way forward seems obscured, fear of failure can breed paralysis. However, practical tactics allow executives to transform unpredictability from an obstacle into a catalyst for possibility.

Rather than waste energy resisting chaos, leaders must acknowledge unpredictability as the default backdrop for decision-making and double down on organizational dexterity. But concrete steps can transform even ambiguous environments from paralyzing hindrances into springboards for creative breakthroughs. Marshalling collective knowledge while responding decisively yet flexibly allows organizations to ride waves of change toward new horizons. Let us examine specific strategies for braving rather than battening down amidst uncertainty.

Strategies for Managing Risk Amidst Uncertainty

1. *Foster Collaboration to See Patterns Faster* – Enhanced stakeholder participation allows identification of emerging opportunities and threats at early stages, granting more time to align strategic response. This mitigates risk by detecting changing currents ahead of manifestations in core metrics. Soliciting diverse inputs also mitigates individual blind spots arising from limited experience or biases. Unified vision builds institutional resilience to navigate unexpected developments.

2. *Adopt Flexible Systems to Enable Quick Shifts* – Rather than committing to rigid solutions vulnerable to disruption, modular frameworks with built-in malleability facilitate rapid recalibration based on real-time data. Standardizing backend processes while localizing front-end delivery enables optimization across locations and segments without wholesale overhaul. Meeting diverse needs through customizable offerings makes change an organizational ally rather than adversary, reducing associated risk.

3. *Design Ongoing Experiments to React Quicker* – Small, continual tests contain fallout while producing actionable insights to guide ongoing adaptation in dynamic contexts. The "set and forget" approach grows increasingly perilous as disrupting forces reshuffle industries overnight. But regular experimentation and evidence-based iteration promotes organizational dexterity to address emerging threats decisively yet nimbly -- managing risk through informed trial and error when precedents prove unreliable.

4. *Incentivize Reasonable Risk-Taking to Spark Innovation* – Since breakthroughs emerge from untested frontiers, fear of failure breeds stagnation out of step with reality's pace. But protecting reasonable experimentation by judging decisions on sound logic rather than just outcomes encourages ambitious innovation within risk guardrails. Manage new ideas less like stern judge and more like empathetic coach or invested venture capitalist, embracing some shortfalls as the cost of trailblazing progress.

5. *Maintain Financial Flexibility for Emergency Pivots* – Success often encourages undisciplined spending and rigid leverage unprepared for sudden reversals. But retaining slack resources enables rapid response to both unexpected headwinds and fleeting opportunities. Conservative budgeting, lean operations, accessible capital and contingency funds empower leaders to maneuver through crisis – transforming

uncertainty from a liability into a catalyst.

6. Game Disruption Scenarios to Get Ahead of Threats – No modern industry remains immune to seismic shake-ups as innovations transform consumer behavior practically overnight, turning stalwarts into has-beens. But envisioning your own disruption equips you to get ahead of change rather than fall behind it. Study wide-ranging trends, run scenario planning exercises, and stress test existing models to uncover signals of impending threats or uncover possibility amidst uncertainty.

To avoid uncertainty's risks causing retreat or ruin, leaders must adopt proactive mindsets and mechanisms to not only endure but even harness change for progress. With informed foresight, adaptable structures, and emergency preparedness, organizations can navigate unpredictable waters fearlessly by transforming disruption's risks into rewards. The way forward may not always be clear, but with the right equipment and crew, stormy seas can be traversed toward new and abundant lands ready to be claimed. Leaning into uncertainty with strategy and spirit positions leaders to ride out passing storms and catch favorable gusts towards horizons of innovation and growth through risk's veils.

The OODA Loop and the Decision Cycle

Business and battle share undeniable parallels. Executives and generals alike must assess ambiguous information, weigh potential moves, and act decisively amidst chaos. Both fields deploy terminology evoking wartime experience like "preemptive strikes," "strategic maneuvers," and "competitive intelligence." This crossover reveals core similarities in making choices under fire. By examining battlefield decision-making models, business leaders can enhance their capacity to think clearly and move quickly within turbulent environments.

One approach proving effective across military, aviation, and entrepreneurial contexts is the OODA Loop - or decision cycle. Developed by US Air Force strategist Colonel John Boyd, this framework rapidly processes changing data to spur action. Just as fighter pilots must observe, orient, decide, and act faster than opponents to dominate in aerial dogfights, executives can "get inside competitors' loops" by accelerating their own cognitive cycles. Examining this model's background and mechanics equips leaders to respond fluidly amidst uncertainty.

History - Air Combat & Quick Thinking

Boyd built his rapid decision framework upon studies of air combat between American and Soviet planes in the Korean War. Specifically, he analyzed why the US F-86 Sabre proved more successful than the opponent's faster, more agile MiG-15s. He determined superior visibility enabled US pilots to quickly process environmental information and initiate moves forcing rivals to react slower. By leveraging this observer advantage, they disabled adversaries cognitively through speed and unpredictability.

Boyd realized such feedforward thinking and fluid responses also drove success beyond aerial battles. Fast and frequent sense-making loops would allow leadership across fields including business, politics, law, and athletics to seize initiative and force errors by overwhelmed competitors. Streamlined observation-to-action shortened response time across diverse strategic contexts from marketing to manufacturing. Thus the OODA loop's relevance exceeds its martial origins, offering a widely applicable decision cycle model.

The Decision Cycle In Practice

The OODA Loop provides a four-phase process for continuous updating and adaptation. By quickly flowing through successive stages, leaders maintain real-time awareness and action faster than change itself. The model comprises:

Observe - Gather wide-ranging data from all sources to identify events affecting status quo. Ask questions to check predictions and surface differing realities across categories like competitors, economics, technology, regulations, demographics.

Orient - Analyze information to determine situational meaning. But acknowledge personal biases filtering interpretations based on experiences, values etc. Speed objectivity by seeking additional perspectives confirming or challenging conclusions.

Decide - Form hypothesis about appropriate strategic responses. Treat choices as fluid works-in-progress subject to ongoing reformulation not rigid attachment.

Act - Implement initial decisions prepared to update actions based on new inputs. Begin observing impact while executing to enable course correction.

Benefits - Speed And Control

Fluid looping through OODA equips leaders to orient quicker and act faster amidst uncertainty. Accelerating the decision cycle is key - shortened lag between observation and adaptation drives proactivity. This inside-out approach forces rivals into reaction mode diminishing their control. Additional benefits include:

- Faster awareness of threats and opportunities before fully formed.

- Quicker understanding of implications through pattern recognition.

- Rapid prototyping of strategic responses via incremental choices.

- Increased innovation through testing multiple flexible hypotheses.

- More resilience via decentralized modular decision authority.

Ultimately OODA compounds speed - the rate of cycling not just choosing. Smooth transitions between steps maintain initiative over events not just competitors. Aligning action to emergent realities grants influence over outcomes.

Businesses must navigate unpredictable waters filled with hidden threats, unexpected gusts, and momentary openings. Like pilots, executives can dominate turbulence by thinking in fluid loops not fixed lines. The OODA model's ability to process ambiguous signals into decisive action represents a competitive advantage whenever outcomes remain in doubt. By accelerating their loops, leaders can gain the upper hand over both disruptive environments and rivals frozen by uncertainty. The fog of business is here to stay, but the decision cycle offers a compass to navigate forward with clarity and power.

Implementing the Decision Cycle

The OODA Loop serves dynamic utility across strategic contexts, equipping users to smoothly adapt choices to ever-changing conditions. But practical application requires more than abstract understanding. Leaders must integrate fluid decision-making into organizational culture through specific methods. Rather than a linear checklist, the loop operates as a continuous flow. Acceleration through tighter iteration emerges from training not mapped steps. What does embedded usage look like in practice?

Integrate Observation: Build environmental scanning capabilities to monitor early signals in all directions. Establish communication channels capturing employee observations plus insights from partners, suppliers, investors and customers. Redundant inputs enhance perspective and pattern recognition.

Prioritize Speed: The pace of orienting and re-orienting determines advantage so analytical velocity enables action ahead of market. Set metrics grading how rapidly teams evaluate meaningful signals and generate strategic hypotheses. Celebrate quick cumulative learning over isolated smart choices.

Formalize Hypothesis Testing: Treat decisions as working theories subject to ongoing examination. Embed experimentation by creating formal deviation approval paths for calculated risks. Ensure teams quickly update choices based on real-world feedback rather than rigid attachment. Make admitting missteps psychologically safe to encourage iterative advancement.

Emphasize Agility: Smooth flow between steps matters more than isolated quality since environments evolve quickly. If observations require extensive discussion before altering direction, adaptation lags reality. Structure roles, responsibilities and rules to avoid bureaucratic lag by empowering dynamic reactions.

Incentivize Cognitive Speed: Recognition, orientation and adaptation represent learnable skills strengthened via practice. Include cycle speed assessments in training programs and performance reviews. Praise first proposed paths fitting facts at time of choosing rather than retroactive "right guesses" since luck invites complacency.

By infusing OODA rhythm into operations, the loop's ongoing momentum supersedes one-off wins. Progress flows from perpetual motion balancing action and information. Integrate the cycle as regenerative business DNA and accelerated decisions will compound gains over time.

Key Takeaways and Final Thoughts on Embracing Uncertainty in Leadership

Key Takeaways:

- Leaders tend to underestimate uncertainty by overestimating their ability to forecast best and worst case scenarios. True unpredictability pervades all complex systems.

- Strategies like seeking diverse inputs, structuring iterative experiments, and focusing on process over outcomes build organizational resilience when navigating ambiguity.

- Cross-collaborative observation helps identify threats and opportunities early while modular flexible systems enable quick response. Reasonable risk-taking fuels innovation within guarded rails.

- The OODA Loop decision cycle promotes fluid adaptation through faster looping between situation assessment, orienting interpretation, deciding on iterative actions, and acting on updated assumptions.

- Accelerated looping builds proactive momentum, forcing rivals into reactive mode. Practical adoption requires cultural integration with incentives and metrics valuing rate over isolated perfection.

Navigating Turbulence Through Collective Decision Agility

This exploration revealed core challenges and tactics for progressing amidst perpetual uncertainty and risk. Accepting overconfidence in prediction allows releasing the futile search for complete data in favor of collective sense-making. Diverse inputs widen perspective on plausible scenarios. Rapid experimentation contains risk while generating strategic insights.

But integrating such principles into organizational DNA proves vital for managing turbulence. The OODA Loop provides helpful scaffolding to accelerate observation, orientation, decisions and actions in smooth succession. Tight iteration maintains initiative over both disruptive shifts and reactionary competitors. Infusing this rhythm across operations builds momentum through cumulative learning and correction.

Yet adoption cannot remain abstract theory or isolated usage. Leaders must nurture collaborative decision agility culturally through training, incentives for cognitive speed, and modular systems empowering fluid responses. The process matters more than perfection. With unified commitment to navigating complexity and emboldened experimentation, groups gain the capacity to redirect even mid-flight towards opportunity.

The pace of change will only accelerate, but the tools for progress remain constant - where will you steer your crew today and how swiftly will they execute the turn? The navigation instruments stand ready should you choose to use them.

Chapter Three

Time Management in Leadership

Time is the most valuable and scarce resource for leaders. Though we all share the confines of 24 hours in a day, how we utilize that time determines our ability to achieve personal and organizational success. This truth applies not just in our personal lives, but profoundly shapes the productivity, performance, and potential of the institutions we lead.

Leadership is fundamentally about effective decision-making concerning strategy and resources. And time, though intangible, is the resource that enables execution of all other strategic plans and goals. As such, time management sits right at the heart of impactful leadership. How well we manage time ripples out to impact our team's effectiveness, the efficiency of organizational processes, and ultimately organizational performance.

This chapter explores why time management matters so much for contemporary organizational leaders, provides frameworks for understanding where leaders often lose time, and offers research-backed strategies to enhance time management at both individual and enterprise-wide levels. Let's begin by understanding just why time has become the currency of successful twenty-first century leadership.

The Accelerated Pace of Business in Digital Contexts

All leaders today operate in a context characterized by exponentially expanding access to information, rapidly evolving workplace tech stacks, and an increasingly global and interconnected marketplace. Information travels and goes out of date quicker than ever before. Attention spans shrink and digital distractions proliferate. Business itself happens at a faster clip, with product cycles compressed and disruptions commonplace.

Leaders have to navigate this accelerated reality and guide their teams and organizations to keep pace. The speed imperative places new pressures on leadership decision-making concerning strategy, innovation, and talent. In this landscape, no organization can afford leisurely deliberations or delayed execution. And employees have heightened expectations of information access, rapid iterations, and agile pathways for idea sharing.

At an individual level, this context demands that leaders become ruthless optimizers of their most scarce resource – time. Every delay in making decisions, every drawn-out and diffuse meeting eats directly into the organizational capacity for nimble innovation essential to flourish amidst digital disruption. As leaders, the way we budget and utilize time has cascading implications for organizational success.

Why We Lose Time: The Enemies of Effective Time Utilization

In their seminal paper, "Actions Speak Louder than Words", researchers explored why knowledge workers average less than 3 hours of productive work daily. By tracking time utilization and categorizing activities, they revealed what really makes up an average workday. Their empirical study exposes three primary "enemies" that routinely hijack leadership time:

1. *Information Overload and Fractured Attention:* Incessant pings of email, an overload of info across communication channels, and the lure of the Internet chews up almost 50% of knowledge workers'

time. With attention fractured, leaders lose time to constant context-switching between tasks.

2. *Poor Prioritization and Diffused Focus:* Instead of channeling efforts on mission-critical priorities, leaders expend time on routine operational tasks better suited for delegation. Lack of strategic clarity on goals or poor prioritization leaves days filled with busyness but little real progress.

3. *Distraction and Interruption:* Open floor plans and a culture of unnecessary meetings fosters constant peer interruption. Each time a task gets interrupted, almost 15 minutes gets lost just restoring focus. Soon half the day is gone.

The way forward lies not in trivial workplace hacks, but in fundamentally shifting leadership time management strategy at personal, team, and enterprise-wide levels. Let's explore research-backed principles to make every minute count.

Strategic Time Management: Making Every Minute Count

The first step lies in leaders adopting an empowered view of time as a strategic asset to optimize, not as an unchangeable reality they are victim to. This means getting clear on personal productivity metrics, auditing current time investments, and having courageous conversations with teams about respecting time boundaries.

At an individual level, leaders must ruthlessly cut out activities adding limited value and those that can be delegated. For everything else, implement focused execution in short intervals by:

1. Batching similar tasks to limit context-switching loss.

2. Setting sharply defined objectives for each work session with metrics for success.

3. Minimizing external and internal interruption during work sessions.

4. Building in strategic buffer time between sessions.

Equally, leaders must foster a culture that respects time across the organization by:

1. Modelling disciplined calendaring, promptness in meetings, and respect for team member time.

2. Establishing organization-wide expectations on email and meeting etiquette and pushing back against time-sucking traditions.

3. Investing in sane technology, calm spatial design, remote or flexible policies to contain productivity killers.

4. Building employee skills on attention management, prioritization, delegation, and strategic procrastination.

The Way Forward: Valuing Time Investment

Legendary management thinker Peter Drucker noted that "Time is the scarcest resource and unless it is managed, nothing else can be managed." As leaders navigate an accelerated and intensely competitive business landscape, every single minute matters both individually and collectively. Just as accounting principles track financial investments, leadership today demands a rigorous approach to tracking and optimizing time investment.

While operational excellence relies on maximizing capital, materials, and labor, the new strategic differentiator lies in expanding innovation capacity, agility to respond to disruption, and complexity management. The road to levelling up on these capabilities runs through smart time investment at scale.

Leaders who embrace this reality and foster a culture grounded in respect for this scarce shared resource will gain the edge. The future belongs to organizations that optimize the asset of time across strategy setting, execution, and innovation. Will you lead the way?

Focused Leadership

Leadership is fundamentally about directing attention - both our own and that of our teams. Where we place our focus as leaders has cascading implications for organizational culture, strategy, and performance. This article explores why attention matters so profoundly for contemporary leaders and provides research-backed frameworks to master three key attentional skills - focusing inward to lead yourself, focusing on others to lead your team, and focusing outward to lead the organization. Let's begin by understanding why focus sits at the heart of impactful leadership.

Leading is not just about vision setting or strategizing. At its core, leadership entails guiding attention across all levels - what issues leaders pay attention to, who they listen to, which ideas they amplify. This ability to direct attention regulates information flow in organizations and signals priorities. As leaders focus on selected signals amidst informational chaos, they cue their teams to do the same.

Equally, leadership presence stems from directing your own attention deliberately. Self-awareness, emotional intelligence, and the capacity to tune out distractions arise from inward attentional mastery. Research reveals that excellent leaders exhibit a signature triad of attentional skills. Let's explore in depth.

Focus Inward: The Lens of Self-Awareness

"Know thyself" - this profound insight sits at the heart of impactful leadership. Self-awareness provides leaders an inner clarity that guides decision-making. It requires directing attention inward to decode our own mental, emotional and physiological signals. Prominent leadership thinker Peter Drucker noted that "you cannot manage other people unless you manage yourself first."

Cultivating Self-Awareness

Recent neuroscience research reveals that we focus inward through interoception - the ability to sense inner physiological cues from heartbeat to respiration. People more able to tune into these signals have greater confidence in their intuitive instincts. Additionally, self-awareness needs us to integrate life experiences into an authentic self-narrative. This demands being open to candid feedback from others, noticing social cues, and recalibrating self-perception.

The payoffs for self-directed leaders are immense. Longitudinal research by leading institutions like Stanford demonstrates that leaders high on self-awareness inspire greater loyalty, are seen as more effective by superiors as well as team members, and enable stronger organizational performance.

Strengthening Willpower - Self-awareness lays the foundation for one of the most vital executive functions - self-control. Also called willpower or cognitive control, this refers to the capacity to pursue goals by managing unruly emotions and tuning out temptation. Studies famously show that self-control measured in children predicts life outcomes even decades later - from financial and health metrics to career success and law-abidance.

The science is clear: stretching willpower like a muscle boosts results. Deliberately testing mental endurance through challenges like avoiding distractions or moderating behaviors helps strengthen cognitive control. Organizations today need leaders with the resilience to handle uncertainty. The road to steering through disruption starts from within through self-mastery.

Focus on Others: The Responsibility of Relationships

Leadership does not occur in a vacuum. At its heart lies understanding both individuals and groups you seek to motivate towards shared goals. Leaders able to direct their attention to build social awareness and empathy gain superior interpersonal dexterity.

Cultivating Cognitive Empathy – Empathy is an overloaded term - however contemporary models distinguish between three scientifically validated types.

Of these, Cognitive empathy creates organizational impact by enabling leaders to stand in another's shoes when communicating. It entails deliberately imagining differing perspectives - an antidote to self-absorption that improves listening and explanation.

Research by leading institutions like Yale demonstrates cognitive empathy to be the strongest predictor of dynamic leadership qualities from selflessness to inspiration of loyalty in teams.

Strengthening Social Sensitivity – Equally, the rapid pace of contemporary business underscores leaders accurately mapping informal networks, relationships, and unwritten norms. Such social sensitivity arises from neural circuits that tune into contextual cues and guide etiquette. Distressingly, research reveals that hierarchical status often impairs this ability even as it becomes more vital.

The counter lies in deliberately shifting attention to lower-ranking colleagues by sustaining eye contact, ensuring responsiveness, and suppressing interruption urge. Simply recording and analyzing speed of response times to team member emails can reveal blind spots! Soft skills drive hard results. Social intelligence separates thriving leaders from lagging ones.

Focus Outward: The Marketplace of Possibilities

Finally, stellar leadership requires expanding focus beyond the inbox clutter to sense the heartbeat of opportunity in your business ecosystem. Leaders tuned out to signals from periphery risk missing game-changing moments. Directing attention outward lays the foundation of vision and strategic thinking.

Cultivating Vigilance – The famed military strategist Sun Tzu noted that "knowledge about the enemy can come only from oneself." Truly focusing outward starts from listening inwards to minimize assumptions before scanning the horizon. It requires cultivating open and vigilant modes of attention through diverse exposures. Serial innovators hold such childlike curiosity. Vigilance then guides what data merits further spotlight through selective attention.

Organizations like Apple show that devil-in-details leaders with wide contextual grasp identify unseen markets. Who you spend time studying shapes the playing field you then seek to transform.

Strengthening Systems Thinking – Focusing outwards pays exponentially huge dividends for leaders integratively connecting contextual dots. Often called systems thinking, this interlinked perspective unveils opportunities through synthesis. Yet systems analysis alone creates lopsided teams. Accentuating emotional intelligence remains imperative to balance and leverage wider viewpoints.

Where focus goes, energy flows and results show. Contemporary leaders face an economy of attention scarcity and information overload unprecedented in history. Exploring frontiers demands channeling collective attention amidst this jungle. The way forward entails deliberately training our mental muscles for self-awareness, empathy and contextual clarity.

Prioritizing Tasks for Maximum Impact

Prioritization is a vital skill that separates good leaders from great ones. At its heart, leading a team means directing attention and resources towards goals that matter most. Everything from meeting deadlines to boosting engagement depends on how well we prioritize collective work. This article dives into prioritization frameworks tailored for project leaders guiding teams handling complex deliverables. Let's first understand why mastering prioritization creates organizational impact.

Why Prioritization Matters

Many project leaders wrongly see prioritization as an operational or tactical concern. But make no mistake - it is profoundly strategic. Flawed prioritization cascades into tangible consequences:

- Lost productivity from misaligned tasks

- Lopsided or delayed outputs

- Disengaged teams from unclear goals

- Time sink in redundant work

The leader's role lies not just in strategic thinking but in guiding execution. And crisp prioritization provides that bridge between vision and making it happen on ground. It acts like a compass guiding team attention amidst noise and uncertainty. Master this hidden skill, and your project leadership transforms.

Challenges in Prioritization

However, optimal prioritization is easier said than done. Project ecosystems tend to be fluid and unpredictable with dependencies that amplify complexity. Both over and under-engineering can distort priorities. Common leadership traps include:

- Signalling everything as urgent, soon nothing is

- Valuing only immediate work, losing sight of goals

- Failing to revisit priorities as new data emerges

- Succumbing to the loudest voice rather than highest value

So what separates the amenability of novices from the mastery demonstrated by stellar project leaders? Deliberate frameworks tailored to handle complexity. Let's break down research-validated principles.

Principle 1: Categorize Across Value and Urgency

Imagine looking at your overflowing inbox and myriad waiting requests. How do you make sense of what matters most? The first step lies in categorizing tasks across two key metrics - value and time sensitivity.

Here is a simple 2 x 2 matrix every project leader should use:

High Value/Urgent: Crisis tasks with tight deadlines - drop everything to handle
High Value/Not Urgent: Critical path tasks, strategic goals - fix protected time
Low Value/Urgent: Time-sensitive busywork - delegate or downgrade
Low Value/Not Urgent: Nice-to-have items - dump/deprioritize

This segmentation clears the fog and provides a blueprint for action. Clarity on what can wait and what can't de-stresses team execution.

Principle 2: Link Priorities to Wider Mission

Your team wants to see meaning in their work, not just mechanically check boxes. Beyond categorizing tasks, take time to link deliverables to the big picture organizational mission. Address how a particular priority ties into team aspirations or stakeholder needs.

Research shows that teams deeply connect goals when leaders frame importance around purpose and potential impact. Inspire pride by noting how excelling on current priorities can showcase team talent. Helping members see the why behind the what hugely uplifts engagement.

Principle 3: Continually Recalibrate

The dynamics of complexity also demand building a feedback loop between priorities, emergent obstacles and new inputs from the ground.

Schedule periodic checkpoints where you reevaluate priorities as a team when changed circumstances demand. Keep an ear out for red flags from members on feasibility. Guide discussions around resource and bandwidth constraints.

Leading amidst uncertainty requires continually listening in and course correcting rather than rigidly sticking to outdated plans. Project management is a team sport - foster transparency around recalibration.

Priority as Leadership Impact Multiplier

Priority setting fundamentally shapes leadership presence on five fronts:

- Signals to organization what - and who - leader values

- Allows delegating the trivial many to focus on vital few

- Enables teams to filter noise and lock into flow states

- Multiplies ability to handle uncertainty and change

- Boosts productivity, performance and collaborative culture

Overcoming Procrastination and Distractions

Procrastination and distraction drain productivity, performance, and potential across organizations. Leaders lose an estimated 70% of time to these common workplace pitfalls that hijack employee attention spans. This epidemic of delay steals precious hours that separate thriving teams from struggling ones.

This article provides a research-backed blueprint to curb procrastination at an individual and organizational level. Let's first explore why beating distraction matters before diving into tactical techniques to foster a culture of executing with excellence.

The Cost of Wasted Time

Procrastination afflicts over 20% of the workforce chronically while nearly all employees lose productive hours daily to distractions. The costs of this wasted time and delayed execution run deep, including:

- Lost productivity from disjointed workflow

- Suboptimal work quality with rushed outputs

- Increased stress and fatigue leading to turnover

- Missed market opportunities from lagging execution

Beyond output metrics, procrastination erodes leadership credibility, accountability, and organizational resilience to handle uncertainty. Thus addressing root drivers merits a strategic intervention.

Why We Delay: Understanding Procrastination Triggers

Changing behaviors first requires decoding why they manifest. Common triggers for workplace procrastination include:

Fear of Failure: Anxiety often paralyzes employees handed ambitious or unclear tasks. Apprehension about capabilities makes it safer not to start rather than risk an imperfect draft.

Low Motivation: Tasks seen as boring, repetitive, or disconnected from individual goals struggle to engage employee attention and energy. Distraction becomes enticing allurement.

Feeling Overwhelmed: Workloads exceeding bandwidth foster panic rather than planning. Faced with a deluge of priorities, people freeze as no single task feels possible to address meaningfully.

Thrill-Seeking: For some temperaments, impending deadlines supply adrenaline that unlocks peak performance. Risk-taking feeds off impending catastrophe rather than planning to prevent it.

Now that we recognize why distraction tempts and delay defers, let's explore proven techniques to overcome these obstacles.

Strategic Framework to Defeat Distraction

1. Set Clear Managerial Expectations

Leaders play a pivotal role in cultivating distraction-resistant cultures by setting clear expectations. For far too long organizations have bemoaned declining attention spans while doing little to formally address hyper-stimulation work contexts.

Start by defining policies on meeting etiquette, email/IM usage, and heads-down time. Celebrate the sanctity of calendars by modeling promptness and preparation. Guide teams on appropriate working hours and reform excessive demand cultures.

Expanding organizational focus beyond outputs to encompass how work gets done fosters transparency and trust. Employees gain permission to build productive rhythms when leaders walk the talk on healthy productivity.

2. Adopt Individual Planning Rituals

However, defeating distraction ultimately starts from individual rituals and routines. Top performers plan in depth to optimize rather than meander haphazardly.

A key differentiator lies in how they structure days. Employ proven frameworks likes time-chunking heavy cognitive tasks while spacing lighter items across days to sustain energy. Set clear priorities ruthlessly excluding the trivial many while protecting hours for the vital few.

Equally, optimize tempo by calibrating on chronotype strengths. Task variety sustains interest while smoothing productive flow states. Inject buffer time between back-to-back meetings and build in preemptive breaks to refresh. Don't overpromise timelines due to optimism or pressure.

Such granular and grounded plans transform employee experience, output and organizational culture. Leaders who role model such mindfulness about time use and task planning build credibility.

3. Strengthen Self-Regulation Skills

However, despite best-laid plans, distraction still arises. Procrastination often stems not from laziness but inadequate self-regulation skills - the ability to monitor thoughts, emotions and behaviors. Building mental muscle and willpower makes it easier to notice unhealthy patterns and deliberately shift gears.

Begin by tracking time investments to reveal waste and trigger points. Test focus by attempting deep work intervals while removing digital distraction. Set micro-goals tied to intrinsic desires versus external validation to sustain motivation. Celebrate small acts of self-care that enable resilience such as meditation, exercise or reflection.

In an economy valuing innovation, creativity and complexity management, organizations can scarcely afford lost hours. Businesses that build cultures empowering employees to immerse in flow states will flourish amid volatility.

However, workforce transformation starts with leadership commitment to cascading focus. Make time utilization data transparent, foster healthy productivity conversations without stigma and reward self-mastery. Give employees both autonomy over attention and accountability for outputs.

The Myth of Multitasking

"Work smarter, not harder" gets touted as sage advice across organizations seeking to raise productivity amidst intensifying workplace complexity. However, buying into the myth of "effective multitasking" achieves the exact opposite by diminishing focus, delaying delivery and straining mental health. This article busts common yet mistaken assumptions leaders hold about multitasking while providing science-backed strategies to foster cultures where uninterrupted attention thrives. Let's first debunk why the brain actually can't multitask before exploring practical alternatives leaders can role model instead.

Why Our Brains Can't Multitask

Multitasking might seem intuitive in an age of unprecedented access to information, rapid context-switching and increased workplace fragmentation. However, neuroscience reveals a fundamental bottleneck - the human brain did not evolve to multitask, only to single-task.

Rather than parallel processing, what happens in multitasking is rapid toggling between tasks. Technically called "task switching", the prefrontal cortex shifts attention between competing stimuli resulting in three tangible consequences:

1. Productivity Loss: Frequent context switching massively cuts into usable time by incurring heavy switch costs - up to 40% decrement across metrics!

2. Quality Erosion: Split attention multiplies errors and allows critical information slippage while decision making suffers from overwhelmed cognitive load.

3. Health Drain: Flitting between tasks tires out executive function similar to decision fatigue. This manifests as burnout, irritability and poorer memory retention.

Now that we recognize why multitasking hampers productivity, let's address common myths that perpetrate unhealthy workplace behaviors.

Myth 1: We Can Train Our Brains to Multitask

Despite feeling increasingly adept at context-switching, no amount of practice actually improves multitasking ability either in accuracy or speed. Studies found people's perception of their effective multitasking had zero correlation with actual capability measured objectively!

Why does it feel easier then? Saliency bias. Being distracted or slowing down feels less visible than before relative to our elevated baseline stress. Don't confuse coping for competence!

Myth 2: Multitasking Saves Time by Increasing Output

Another assumption is that doing multiple things simultaneously boosts work throughput overall, even accounting for inefficiency. However data shows the exact opposite!

By impairingworkflows, multitasking increases total time needed significantly in addition to the final work requiring heavy revisions or remaining incomplete! Consequently deadlines slip, not shorten. Leaders who encourage a culture fixated on speed inadvertently undermine it through fragmentation.

Myth 3: Media Multitasking During Down Time is Harmless

Perhaps the most pernicious myth is that casual media multitasking during downtime at work is harmless stress relief. Research indicates otherwise.

Rapid app switching corrodes concentration span making it harder to resume focused workflows. Worse, habitual media distraction impairs both short and long term memory formation while increasing proneness to errors - destroying productivity well past the break!

Cultivating Focus: Leadership Strategies Beyond Multitasking

Streamlining attention is a competitive advantage in the economy of ideas. The path forward lies in modeling and encouraging focus augmenting behaviors organization-wide:

1. Ruthlessly Audit Distractions: Self-audit what triggers pointless media toggling during work before removing apps. Build system-wide visibility into collaboration platforms dismissing redundant ones.

2. Formally Reinforce Focus: Institute reasonable policies on meeting punctuality, email availability and heads-down time. Incentivize leaders to take breaks without devices over constant partial attention.

3. Empower Focused Roles: Foster ROI evaluation of individual contributor roles needing deep concentration. Enable workflow support through guarded calendars and minimal meetings.

A key leadership responsibility lies in shaping cultures centered around time as the most valuable asset. Multitasking erodes this scarce collective resource for marginal gains in speed but significant losses in impact. The myth promises more but hampers human potential. However, leaders mindful about depth, duration and protection of attention build organizations resilient against fragmentation.

Key Takeaways and Final Thoughts on Time Management in Leadership

Key Takeaways:

- Leaders face an accelerated pace of business amidst digital disruption, demanding ruthless optimization of the scarce resource of time through attentional mastery at individual and organizational levels.

- Focused leadership entails deliberately training mental muscles for self-awareness, empathy and contextual clarity to guide strategy setting and execution.

- Effective prioritization provides a bridge between vision and execution by directing collective attention on goals that matter most amidst uncertainty.

- Curbing distraction and procrastination requires addressing root cultural triggers and equipping employees with techniques for self-regulation.

- Embracing "mono-tasking" mindsets maximizes productivity over the myth of multitasking which erodes quality through fragmented attention.

Directing Focus in an Age of Distraction: Time Management as Strategic Leadership

Across industries, leadership now occurs against a backdrop of unprecedented access to information, rapidly evolving workplace technology, and an intensely competitive global marketplace. As leaders navigate this landscape, one scarce yet precious asset emerges as key to unlocking organizational potential: attention.

Leaders bear responsibility for directing attention across multiple fronts - focusing inward for self-awareness, focusing on understanding others, and focusing outward to scan the horizon. Excellence on each vector shapes institutional strategy setting and execution.

In such environments characterized by information overload and exponential complexity, the fundamental leadership challenge lies in ruthlessly optimizing the resource of time. How leaders budget and utilize their own and collective attention has a force-multiplying impact on performance.

This chapter has highlighted science-backed insights for leaders seeking to hone an organization's competitive edge through strategic time investment. The way forward entails deliberately training our mental muscles on critical attentional skills - prioritization, focus, and minimizing distractions.

With crisp understanding of cultural triggers and individual mastery over attention, leaders can foster execution orientation and amplify productivity. As the pace of business accelerates, the future belongs to organizations centered around uncommon clarity on what matters most.

Chapter Four

A Strategic Approach to Effective Meetings

Meetings play a pivotal role in organizations, serving as gatherings where information is shared, decisions are made, and execution strategies are formed. However, we have all likely experienced the frustration of wasted time in pointless meetings that spur little action or progress. As leaders, how can we transform meetings into productive engines that align teams and drive organizational success? The key lies in intentionally structuring meetings to extract value from each participant.

I propose applying three critical questions, which I refer to as the "Three Yields of Effective Meetings," to evaluate if a meeting achieves an acceptable return on investment of participants' time and company resources:

1. What did I learn?

2. What did I contribute?

3. What do I do next?

If participants can respond with clear, tangible answers for each question, the meeting has succeeded for them and, in turn, for the organization. However, if attendees leave without learning anything new, adding any insights, or understanding their next steps, the gathering has failed to utilize their skills and knowledge to move key priorities forward. As management expert Peter Drucker noted, "Meetings are by definition a concession to deficient organization. For one either meets or one works. One cannot do both at the same time." With intentional planning, the Three Yields model provides a framework for leaders to shift meetings from an operational deficiency to a strategic asset.

The Three Yields questions equip leaders with a simple yet powerful diagnostic to determine who truly needs to participate in a meeting versus who may simply want to attend for other reasons. For instance, the "just in case" syndrome manifests when executives bring any team member or bag carrier who worked on a project or task, regardless of their ability to meaningfully contribute during the discussion. While understandable in some contexts, this tendency bloats meetings with attendees who have little to add. It can also indicate deficiencies in leadership, as executives should command the knowledge to address key questions about major initiatives without relying on silent subordinates in the room.

Relatedly, some junior team members suffer from "face time" syndrome - an erroneous belief that passive attendance during meetings with senior leaders can advance their careers, regardless of their contributions. However, as leadership expert John C. Maxwell outlines, "Leadership develops daily, not in a day." Simply occupying space in high-level meetings without using one's voice breeds stagnation rather than growth for emerging leaders. Additionally, senior executives want to catalyze productive dialogue and decisions, not manage spectator events.

Applying the Three Yields line of questioning helps distinguish professionals who can drive a discussion from observers who divert focus. As Harvard Business School professor Michael Roberto notes, excessive attendees without a clear purpose muffle productive debate, as "a broader range of alternatives is discussed when the group is smaller." A leadership team has no need for spectators when strategic priorities are at stake.

The Three Yields framework centers meetings around participant value over organizational custom. Indeed, research found that many questionable meetings persist simply due to legacy reasons versus purposeful design. Rather than accepting a vague agenda, leaders should consider:

- What do we want each attendee to learn?

- What unique insights can they contribute?

- And how will this gathering equip them with clarity to execute next steps?

Leadership teams can no longer use meetings as catch-all containers for organizational needs without structural intent. The Three Yields questions demand focused agendas on precise issues with measurable returns.

Leaders play a stewardship role over one of any organization's scarcest resources - employee time. A 2022 Microsoft survey found that unnecessary meetings cost enterprises $399 billion annually in lost productivity. As each meeting convenes numerous professionals and coordinates even more with calendaring, a single misaligned gathering has exponential impact. Applying the Three Yields meeting evaluators safeguards against wasted energy, preserving time for roles that align with attendees' strengths and organizations' highest priorities. Indeed, a focused meeting energizes teams around meaningful objectives, whereas an unclear gathering demoralizes with ambiguity.

An intentional approach to curating meetings is no longer an operational luxury - it is a strategic mandate in a competitive employment market where professionals enjoy options. Utilizing the Three Yields framework to craft agendas and attendee lists ensures that meetings extract the maximum value from each participant through enrichment, contribution, and execution planning. While called "soft skills," meeting facilitation and team leadership acumen drive hard

ROI. Indeed, as leadership expert Patrick Lencioni wrote, "Meetings are not just the avenue for getting things done. They are the way an organization transforms groups of talented individuals into cohesive teams." Convening the right people in fruitful dialogue moves strategies from ideas to actions - the very fuel of organizational progress. With a structured approach, leaders can shift meetings from operational baggage to high-performance engines designed for meaningful progress.

A Strategic Approach to Planning and Executing Productive Meetings

Few organizational responsibilities demand greater leadership stewardship than coordinating cross-functional teams toward mission-critical results. Meetings serve as vessels carrying precious strategy into the seas of execution, relying on diligent navigation to transport priorities safely through subversive tides seeking to shunt hard-earned progress off course. Indeed, turbulent markets and ever-evolving customer expectations require enterprise-wide coordination through integrated effort and real-time adaption fueled by shared insights.

Unfortunately, like captains on compromised ships, many leaders operate meetings without strategic instrumentation to guide teams through the storm. Despite significant investments of management attention and team talent, research suggests over 67% of organizational meetings fail to catalyze decisions or measurable outcomes, amounting to wasted energy that demoralizes staff momentum. Why do well-intentioned gatherings so often undermine strategic imperatives through misalignment and ambiguity rather than advancing clarity on priorities?

In my experience collaborating with executive teams across industries, meetings falter due to perfunctory planning emphasizing convenience over intentional construction. When leaders architect gatherings merely to satisfy organizational custom rather than activate talent against defined priorities, meetings devolve into aimless theatrics generating more smoke than light. However, by embracing their role as navigators across the enterprise and applying steering instruments intentionally designed to optimize meetings' efficiency and effectiveness, leaders can utilize recurring touchpoints as engines to accelerate mission-critical results.

Shifting from Perfunctory to Purposeful Meeting Planning

Transforming team gatherings into Drivers of progress begins with leaders rejecting reactive approaches to meeting coordination. Rather than allowing organizational gravity toward disengaged convenience to corrupt strategic priorities, we must reclaim meetings as engines of insight exchange and execution alignment centered on defined objectives.

Consider that managers often find themselves trapped in routine meetings loosely scheduled from the previous quarter with no deliberate design modifications to address evolving team needs. Such scenarios reflect dated assumptions that if a meeting held value historically, its current construct must remain automatically valid. However, sharp leaders understand that shifting market realities and team dynamics require continually realigning the purpose, roster, and agenda guiding every gathering.

Before coordinating team time, step back to reexamine fundamental planning questions through a lens of intentional leadership:

- What specific outcomes do we want to achieve from bringing folks together?

- Who truly needs to participate to constructively inform or advance progress?

- How will we design the agenda to extract maximum leadership value from attendees?

Approaching meeting coordination as an instrument of transformation rather than a passive procedure liberates leaders from legacy habits bred by organizational inertia. The work of convening offers tremendous power to determine whether gatherings build strategic capabilities or simply atrophy into repetitive box-checking.

As enterprise leaders, our role involves stewarding scarce resources, especially our team members' precious time and talent. Rather than allowing meetings to denigrate into aimless pageantry, we must challenge ourselves to intentionally develop every gathering. Much like disciplined athletes, leaders must incorporate skills training into collaboration opportunities to expand capacities today that better navigate unpredictable tomorrows. Let us explore constructive frameworks to elevate meeting impact.

Getting Crystal Clear on Desired Outcomes

I have facilitated many gatherings derailed by unclear objectives, evidenced by diffuse dialogue spreading teams thin across tangential topics unrelated to core priorities requiring executable strategies. Such meetings admirably intend to inform and align groups, however ambiguity on desired outcomes inevitably leads to lost opportunities from wasted mindshare targeting theoretical rather than tangible progress.

Leaders can catalyze meetings through outcome clarity by taking a step back to define:

- What specific challenges or performance indicators necessitate this meeting?

- How will we focus team insights on constructing executable strategies versus theoretical exploration?

- What precise products should we complete by gathering's end to advance progress?

An old adage advises "beginning with the end in mind" - wise guidance for engineering leadership meetings as accelerators of strategic priorities. Defining the intended milestones ahead grounds teams in navigational purpose rather than simply boarding aimless vessels set adrift. Furthermore, measurable targets expand creativity by challenging groups to construct innovative pathways aligned to real-world applications.

Examining the Roster with Discerning Eyes

In my experience advising executive teams, leaders often determine meeting rosters based on org charts and formal titles rather than contextual insights required to construct holistic strategies. However, effective collaboration requires factoring in specialized expertise, hands-on experience, and cross-departmental impacts essential for sustainable execution.

Before sending blanket calendar invites, thoughtfully examine:

- Who offers on-the-ground intelligence to reality check assumptions?

- Who provides technical insights or oversees downstream implementation?

- What perspective diversity must we incorporate for comprehensive strategy factors?

Curating a balanced lineup not beholden to hierarchy can shine light on blindspots that undermine execution once teams disband to operational trenches beyond the meeting room. Allow folks with differing vantage points to inform one another rather than isolating leadership to theoretical echo chambers disconnected from real-world complexities.

Architecting an Agenda with Transformational Intent

An ambiguous agenda communicates diffuse priorities bound to derail groups despite best intentions. However, a strategic agenda grounded in real-world outcomes signals the path for aligning insights into progress.

- Sharpen meeting efficiency through structured agendas that designate:

- Framing to establish shared baseline understanding so everyone starts on same page

- Focus Areas defining challenges teams will solve for through multi-dimensional strategies

- Enrichment Insights to broaden thinking and building leadership skills beyond tactical meeting purpose

- Work Products that move priorities forward for downstream implementation

Additionally, punctual gatherings demonstrate respect for participants' time while underscoring preciousness of collaborative opportunities to drive strategic acceleration.

Leading Meetings with Facilitative Finesse

Skilled navigators combine directive steering toward destinations with democratic sail hoisting harnessing diverse insights on optimizing course calibration. Similarly, excellent meeting facilitators balance targeted outcomes against participative inclusivity expanding collective wisdom into executable strategies. Such dexterity enables teams to examine organizational challenges through multidimensional perspectives grounded in real-world dynamics.

Practically speaking, artful facilitation blends:

- Affirmative Listening to extract insights from across groups without allowing dominance by select few

- Tactical Interjection to resolve unproductive tangents threatening agenda focus

- Clear Next Steps summarized to enable downline ownership over priorities in motion

By receiving diverse inputs while guiding teams toward definable implementation plans, leaders can facilitate meetings as engines transforming organizational potential into strategic progress.

Much like championship athletes, outstanding organizations recognize meetings as training grounds to build strategic capabilities converting today's performance into tomorrow's progress. As leaders face quickening market turbulence and complexity, a renewed commitment to convening groups with intentional design offers critical lifelines.

Often the most pragmatic solutions come from connecting insights across functions, experience levels, and roles unable to be unlocked in isolated corners. If leaders fail to spark such creative collisions through purposeful gatherings, siloed strategies inevitably struggle scaling organizational obstacles downstream. However, leaders who intentionally develop meetings as instruments for unlocking collective potential position their teams to nimbly adapt in an ever-changing world.

While occasionally inconvenient in the moment, collaboration through shared challenges weaves connective tissue across the enterprise. May we as leaders pledge renewed gravity over architecting meetings as cornerstones energizing our organization's future. For on the other side of discomfort lives discovery catalyzed through forging teams today ready to excel no matter tomorrow's uncertainties.

Cultivating Inclusion through Intentional Meeting Design

Meetings serve as pillars upholding organizational culture, providing venues for teams to exchange ideas, assess challenges, and construct solutions. However, traditional gatherings often limit diverse contribution through non-inclusive participant dynamics that prioritize dominant voices over marginalized perspectives. Research reveals only 35% of professionals feel consistently empowered to share views in meetings, with women and people of color least likely to contribute. Such narrow expression of talent compromises innovation and overlooks critical insights required for holistic understanding. As companies navigate complex markets, how can leaders transform meetings from theaters of exclusion into engines of inclusion that engage a breadth of voices? The path forward challenges traditional assumptions on gathering practices with inclusive redesign.

Inclusion as a Leadership Imperative

Constructing inclusive meetings begins by reorienting organizational gravity from perfunctory procedures toward equity and access. Leaders must acknowledge that while gatherings intend to inform and align groups, marginalizing conditions structure interaction toward certain voices based on identity, experience and perceived status. Unpacking exclusion requires moving beyond individual behaviors to examine systems that isolate contribution opportunities for minoritized professionals based on dominant norms.

Furthermore, research clearly links inclusive companies with higher performance, creativity and employee retention over less diverse competitors. If organizations only reap such benefits through comprehensive market insights, solutions and leadership approaches, meetings must uplift a chorus of perspectives rather than simply privilege the loudest soloists. Leaders play a profound role in fostering inclusion by cultivating conditions where all contributors can shine.

Architecting Equitable Meetings

Transitioning toward inclusive gatherings first requires replacing assumptions with intentionality. The following practices provide leadership guideposts:

Establish Psychological Safety

Meetings rely on vulnerable exchange between individuals with varying positional powers, experiences and communication styles. Attendees may resist sharing unconventional yet critical perspectives without confidence that such views will receive thoughtful consideration rather than knee-jerk judgment.

Leaders demonstrate credibility through behaviors that foster psychological safety:

- Welcoming new voices instead of only relying on senior personnel

- Drawing out quiet attendees by creating space for multiple views

- Affirming each contributor to encourage ongoing participation

Such leadership body language communicates that all seated around the table offer valued expertise.

Clarify Participation Guidelines

Seemingly natural discussion dynamics often exclude individuals based on identity, style and experience. Leaders must establish participation guidelines that structure equitable contribution opportunities by:

- Discouraging interruptions that cut perspectives short

- Advocating for speakers to finish articulating views before responding

- Calling on marginalized group members directly to include isolated voices

While conversation flows organically when groups share affinity, leaders must spark contribution across difference.

Ensure Agenda Responsiveness

Meetings often follow standardized templates that fail to address emergent needs from diverse groups. Leaders can empower inclusion through adjustable agendas that adapt to arising priorities from meeting participants. Building time for attendee suggestions at gathering outset acknowledges leadership limitations in singularly dictating content. Meetings grounded in shared authority expand beyond the constraints of top-down perspective into landscapes of collective wisdom.

Expand Access through Creative Channels

Every individual holds a unique voice - but not all prefer projecting words across a crowded conference table. Leveraging alternate contribution channels beyond spoken discussion supports inclusion by removing barriers to collaboration:

- Digital polling for real-time perspective gathering

- Anonymous ideation to broaden thinking

- Small group dialogue for risk-taking

By diversifying participation modes, leaders can shrink social distance between roles to benefit from multidimensional expertise within teams.

Realigning Assumptions through Courageous Curiosity

Shifting meetings from venues of exclusion into inclusive innovation hubs requires leaders to courageously examine systems that concentrate power in the hands of privilege. Curiosity moves diversity initiatives beyond tokenism by asking questions that unpack exclusion:

- Whose voices dominate most meetings? Which groups rarely contribute?

- What meeting conditions might isolate marginalized team members?

- How can we nurture psychological safety for minority groups?

- Processing tadpoles of awareness into action requires identifying roots of marginalization that compromise organizational potential through lack of inclusion. Leaders must hold tension between actual and ideal to chart pathways toward equitable collaboration.

The Leadership Opportunity in Architecting Inclusion

Meetings serve as cornerstones upholding organizational culture. However, traditional gatherings often limit contribution through participant dynamics that prioritize dominant voices. As companies navigate increasingly diverse markets, complexity demands leadership approaches that engage a breadth of voices through reinventing meetings as inclusive innovation hubs.

The path toward inclusion relies not on another program but on transformed culture that embraces meetings as instruments for multiplicity over singularity. True change requires replacing assumptions with awareness, empathy with equity. Leadership lives on the other side of discomfort, for beyond tension lies community unlocked when we architect inclusion with courageous curiosity. Our organizations, and our societies, depend on such conscientious bravery.

Assessing Meeting Impact

The true measure of a gathering goes beyond attendance logs and calendar blocks. How can leaders evaluate the tangible impact meetings generate for enterprise strategy and team cohesion? By embracing a results-focused approach, managers can shift meetings from vague activities to defined projects propelling organizational momentum.

Defining Desired Outcomes

Effective meetings run on clarity of purpose and priorities. Without defined goals and success metrics established at the outset, teams risk misguided efforts or distraction by tangents unrelated to business objectives. To catalyze impact, leaders should anchor every gathering by determining:

1. What specific business needs or problems necessitate this meeting?

2. What measurable outcomes should result from this discussion to qualify as success?

3. How will we track progress on defined priorities following the session?

Anchoring team dialogue around concrete objectives circumvents diffusion across too many theoretical topics removed from executable actions. Additionally, a results-focused approach expands creativity by challenging groups to assess practical applications of ideas in relation to real-world needs. Leaders who dedicate time upfront getting crystal clear on desired meeting outputs enable more focused pathways toward constructing impactful solutions.

Monitoring Participant Engagement

From body language to verbal cues, participant engagement serves as a real-time performance indicator on whether meetings achieve resonance. Low energy levels or distracted behaviors signal poor facilitation or misaligned topics divorced from attendee interests. High engagement marked by robust dialogue and collaborative problem-solving confirms meetings as relevant venues for talent activation. Leaders seeking to catalyze impact should monitor engagement by asking:

- Are participants actively contributing insights and expertise to advance key objectives?

- Does the dialogue reflect constructive debate and innovative ideation?

- Are quiet voices drawn out to capture diverse perspectives across the team?

Real-time adjustments to agenda items or facilitation approaches allow leaders to reignite participant investment when engagement lulls. Furthermore, broad contribution across team members produces comprehensive insights to power executable strategies with ownership cultivated at the ground level.

Driving Accountability through Action Plans

The ultimate measure of meetings lies in the executable strategies and leadership decisions they produce to accelerate progress on business objectives. Without clear documentation of agreed-upon plans and defined next steps, meetings risk becoming theoretical exchanges rather than transformation catalysts. To drive accountability, leaders should close each gathering by:

- Reviewing decisions, priorities and work products created by the team

- Clarifying assignments and timelines for advancing key next steps

- Establishing future touch points to track progress and address obstacles

By capturing clear actions in meeting minutes and shared project plans, leaders enable downstream accountability to translate strategic dialogue into tangible outcomes.

Evaluating Efficient Use of Resources

Meetings convene precious leadership assets - an organization's top talent. When coordinated perfunctorily as a matter of routine, meetings waste both human capital and company time. However, when designed intentionally, meetings activate cross-functional teams toward accelerating results. To ensure meetings deliver value worthy of resource investment, leaders should examine:

- Did the gathering produce clear outputs aligned to business objectives?

- Were participants focused on advancing key priorities rather than theoretical dialogue?

- Could we have achieved similar outcomes through other means?

Assessing gathering efficiency safeguards against participant fatigue and ensures collaboration time concentrates on moving the needle on critical goals.

Strengthening Organizational Culture

Meetings provide rare windows where far-flung team members converge to reconnect on vision, values and community. When executed skillfully, meetings can re-energize employee inspiration by revealing progress toward purpose. To leverage gatherings for cultural cohesion, leaders should consider:

- Are participants demonstrating organizational values during discussions?

- Does the dialogue suggest high levels of trust and conflict resolution dexterity?

- Are teams celebrating wins while taking setbacks in stride?

Well-run meetings offer glimpses into organizational culture in action, allowing leaders to take the pulse on morale while shaping norms.

Transforming meetings from passive procedure into active accelerators requires leaders who evaluate impact beyond allocated calendar blocks. By continually realigning gathering objectives, monitoring participant engagement, capturing executable actions, maximizing resource efficiency and shaping culture, managers can amplify meetings as engines that convert insights into outcomes. Though organizational necessity often mandates participation, leadership strategy determines whether teams leverage gatherings to advance priorities or simply bide time. With an intentional approach, leaders can guide meetings from distraction toward destinations where progress waits.

Key Takeaways and Final Thoughts on A Strategic Approach to Effective Meetings

Key Takeaways:

- Clearly define desired outcomes upfront to focus team efforts toward measurable results

- Curate inclusive participation through equitable contributor guidelines fostering psychological safety

- Continuously realign gathering objectives and agendas to address emergent needs

- Capture executable actions in shared documentation to drive downstream accountability

- Evaluate meetings on efficiency and impact to ensure optimal resource allocation

- Monitor engagement levels and culture clues to fine-tune facilitation approaches in real-time

Transforming Team Traction through Strategic Meeting Management

Meetings serve as critical venues for exchanging insights, constructing solutions, and aligning team efforts toward key priorities. However, without intentional design, meetings default to vague activities rather than defined projects propelling organizational momentum. As key stewards over precious company resources like employee time and attention, leaders play an instrumental role in orchestrating high-impact gatherings that accelerate strategic progress.

By clearly defining desired outcomes at the outset, leaders can focus team dialogues on executable actions over theoretical tangents. Additionally, establishing inclusive participation guidelines and equitable contribution models taps into diverse perspectives while providing psychological safety for vulnerable voices. Furthermore, leaders must continually revisit and realign gathering objectives to address emergent needs revealed through external conditions or internal team dynamics. Capturing outcomes and clarifying accountabilities before concluding each meeting drives downstream implementation of identified solutions. Finally, evaluating gatherings based on efficiency and business impact ensures optimal resource allocation toward differentiated results.

The true calling of leadership lives in our capacity to spark human potential toward meaningful progress. As orchestrators over collective talent, meetings offer profound instruments for leaders to shape team culture, facilitate generative dialogue, and transform individual contributors into aligned communities united by shared purpose. By embracing the architect role with strategic intentionality, leaders can guide organizations from disconnected distraction toward destinations where progress waits. For on the other side of mindful gathering lies community unlocked when people come together.

Chapter Five

Strategic Project Leadership

Projects serve a pivotal role in driving strategic change and innovation in organizations. However, between tight budgets, limited resources, shifting priorities and politics, leading complex projects strategically presents multifaceted challenges for managers and executives. Studies indicate that over 50% of organizational projects fail outright or witness dramatic shortfalls between intended goals and actual outcomes. These failures extract steep costs in wasted investments across people, processes and technology amounting to trillions annually.

Why do projects sponsored by experienced leaders in well-run companies still routinely fail? In most cases, deficits in strategic leadership undercut a project's trajectory well before meaningful work even begins. Without proactive measures, otherwise competent leaders can inadvertently introduce flaws that send the endeavor careening off the rails.

Strategic thinkers recognize that projects do not exist in isolation but remain deeply intertwined with the organizational ecosystems in which they operate. Like intricate machines, the constitutive elements of people, information flows, resources and culture must harmonize to drive progress. A breakdown in any area rapidly cascades across the entire system.

In this light, the seasoned leader views projects through a strategic lens that traces complex interdependencies while also serving to identify critical points of strength, weakness and leverage. Armed with this perspective, executives can navigate the following four essential domains to lay foundations that set projects up for success.

Defining the Right Problems & Outcomes

The starting line for any project lies in leadership defining the right problem and associated outcomes. Clarity of purpose serves a centripetal force that aligns efforts while also enabling clear metrics for evaluating progress. Without it, teams operate in a fragmented vacuum generating scattered movement but little forward momentum.

Project leaders should guide teams in clarifying purpose by first understanding problems through the lens of strategic priority amidst competing initiatives. Effective frameworks evaluate the urgency, cost of failure and current traction around a given issue. Teams should tie project outcomes to vital performance indicators for the organization, whether captured numerically or through milestones demonstrating strategic impact.

For example, a technology project may aim to achieve a 20% gain in manufacturing plant productivity over 18 months as increasing throughput remains an urgent priority. Traction around upgrading underlying machinery and systems already shows promise in unlocking capacity constraints. Success directly ties to strategic financial and operational goals, while failure risks declining market share, margins and brand reputation over time.

In contrast, unclear purpose mires projects in ambiguity from day one. Teams thrash about trying to deliver an array solutions without understanding core issues and associated measures for impact. Over time, frustration mounts as expectations and interpretations of what constitutes success vary widely across stakeholders. Momentum evaporates as players openly question the rationale behind the entire endeavor.

By taking the time to deeply clarify purpose, leaders enable teams to focus efforts on the right priorities early while working towards outcomes that best serve organizational strategy. This forms the sturdy scaffolding on which to build execution plans across complex project environments.

Securing Ownership & Authority

With strategic foundations rooted firmly in purpose and priorities, seasoned leaders next focus on empowering the right sponsors who will shepherd projects to success. No endeavor operates in a vacuum insulated from organizational dynamics. A strong sponsor serves to break through barriers, accelerate decisions and remove political roadblocks that inhibit progress.

Effective sponsors occupy positions of influence with access to critical resources and the organizational authority to drive outcomes. They zealously believe in the project purpose and remain willing to battle on the team's behalf. Without steadfast sponsors, projects risk stall-outs whenever encountering technical debates, conflicts over resources or serious setbacks.

For complex projects, fragmentation often occurs as various departments nominally sponsor disparate workstreams. When trouble hits, no clear owner emerges with the influence and willingness to unblock the team. Leaders must take care to clearly designate a single senior executive that retains ultimate ownership and decision rights crucial for pushing through barriers.

A strong sponsor also signals to the organization that a project aligns to top priorities justifying heightened attention and support companywide. Teams backed by C-suite leaders or mission-critical department heads relay strategic importance prompting closer cooperation. In contrast, initiatives sponsored 3 or 4 levels down evoke impressions of mundane or tangential efforts that quickly fall by the wayside as organizational interests inevitably conflict with project needs.

By taking the long view to carefully match projects with qualified sponsors in positions of power, leaders enable the influence and strategic stature necessary for teams to deliver on critical initiatives. With strong sponsors secured, organizations can then determine team composition and governance processes.

Engaging Project Stakeholders Strategically

Project success hinges on leaders continuously nurturing relationships with invested parties through open, tailored communications addressing unique needs and concerns.

Who Qualifies as a Project Stakeholder?

Stakeholders represent individuals and groups substantially impacted by a project's outcomes, either directly or indirectly. Key stakeholders may actively participate on delivery teams as sponsors, customers or vendors while others monitor progress from the sidelines in oversight roles. Regulators, directors and adjacent staff teams qualify as stakeholders when organizational initiatives broadly affect operations.

Communication serves as the lifeblood flowing between project leaders and stakeholders, carrying critical information and enabling dialogue. Fluid exchanges allow teams to align expectations, surface issues early and collect feedback to guide efforts in the right direction. Leaders who overlook communication as a vital project component risk severed connections that ultimately compromise outcomes down the line.

Strategic Communicators Understand Stakeholder Perspectives

Seasoned leaders and communicators recognize that diverse stakeholders arrive with unique histories, objectives and concerns that inform needs. What information matters most? How does the stakeholder prefer to receive updates and share insights? Leaders attuned to these perspectives tailor communications accordingly.

For example, senior executives may care most about high-level progress to budget and strategic goals requiring summaries in familiar financial terminology. Operations teams need detailed briefings on process changes and training requirements well in advance of deployment. Marketing focuses on how product capabilities and messaging get shaped for market.

Meanwhile, vendor interactions concentrate on tactical execution and payments. Regulators monitor compliance to policies and protocols. Each deserves a tailored communications approach.

Beyond retention, strategic leaders also segment stakeholders by influence on the project itself and associated priorities. Key voices can make or break initiatives warranting tighter communications that promptly address worries. Leaders empower outcomes by dedicating additional cycles to influential stakeholder relationships, similar to nurturing key sales prospects.

Establishing Early Connections

Smart leaders commence stakeholder communications right when embarking on strategic initiatives before potential issues escalate. Early exchanges serve several purposes:

- Informing on goals, vision and proposed changes underway

- Educating on anticipated impacts across the organization

- Learning stakeholder needs and concerns

- Discovering opportunities to improve plans and outcomes

- Gathering input on role clarity and ownership

Early transparency around objectives coupled with a genuine willingness to listen earns stakeholder trust in leadership's capability to appropriately guide teams. Leaders gain invaluable insights that help navigate challenges before they become intractable crises.

The Communications Feedback Loop

Communications then continue throughout initiatives through regular touchpoints that keep stakeholders informed on progress and changes while prompting ongoing discussions. Consistent engagement maintains productive relationships and alerts leaders to emerging risks.

For example, a monthly newsletter from the project sponsor quickly briefs all stakeholders on accomplishments, next steps and help needed. Live question and answer webinars every quarter enable deeper discussions especially around thorny issues. Office hours with project principals provide outlets for personalized support. Leaders also setup simple feedback channels including anonymous options that encourage candid inputs.

Meanwhile, one-on-one briefings give influential stakeholders red carpet treatment in exchange for endorphin boosts of wisdom. Smart leaders close each interaction by summarizing key next steps demonstrating accountability. Documenting exchanges likewise keeps records that prevent confusion and disputes down the line should miscommunications unfortunately still occur.

Tune into Nonverbal Cues

Beyond spoken language, seasoned leaders also monitor nonverbal signals and behaviors that offer additional context into stakeholder mindsets. For example, does the executive still exhibit signs of doubt when discussing deployment plans? Did concerns escalate given recent financial performance? Does the manager appear distracted or frequently reschedule briefings? Even small observations provide clues into shifting dynamics that warrant further exploration.

In some cases, leaders may detect overt disengagement as stakeholders grow frustrated, cynical or even hostile towards initiatives underway. Immediate intervention helps to uncover root issues and restore productive working relationships before permanent damage gets inflicted.

Tuning out these critical cues risks allowing small gaps to expand into unbridgeable chasms doomed for conflict. Vigilance paired with empathy keeps leaders connected to stakeholder experiences needed to guide teams successfully towards collective wins.

Adjusting the Channel Dial

Leaders must also regularly reevaluate communications efficacy and fine tune approaches over time as stakeholder needs shift. For example, certain messages may resonate better delivered in-person versus email. Some prefer asynchronous communications allowing self-paced reviewing while others want live interactions. Leaders remain attentive and adaptable to optimize information flows.

During launch phases, social touches that build rapport take precedence. As priorities narrow executing specific project components, task-oriented communications delving into detail proves essential. Leaders dial channels and content appropriately much like a radio DJ changing songs to match the evolving mood.

Stakeholder communication remains a pivotal yet oft neglected component governing project outcomes. Leaders concentrating exclusively on deliverables risk overlooking the diverse people navigating organizational changes together.

By investing in understanding unique perspectives and nurturing connections strategies, leaders add stakeholder courage that uplifts teams over barriers on the journey ahead. All travel further together through strong bonds built on open, tailored and trustworthy communications.

Assembling the Project Team

Seasoned leaders understand that a team's capabilities prove integral to project success and anchor efforts early on to secure top talent. Studies clearly demonstrate that a motivated team exhibiting diverse strengths significantly outperforms groups of average ability or homogenously skilled members.

In high performer teams, individuals across functions apply their expertise towards shared goals covering the range of competencies needed for superior outcomes. For example, a team integrating a new data analytics platform requires fluent speakers across business operations, technical architecture, project management and change leadership. Together, they anticipate multi-faceted challenges that single discipline groups often miss.

Complex projects demand even greater diligence to talent as needs intensify around specialized skills and navigating uncertainty. Subpar resourcing inevitably handicaps initiatives from the start as gaps appear in delivering quality solutions or managing stakeholders skillfully. Progress stalls quickly as morale and momentum nosedives across overtaxed teams struggling with inadequate capabilities.

Unfortunately, executives often gravitate towards convenience and availability when staffing endeavors rather than making the hard resourcing decisions needed to secure top professionals. Allowances get made when department heads push back on releasing top talent "due to conflicting priorities". Leaders may also gravitate towards more junior resources as veterans occupy senior operational roles.

While expedient in the moment, these rationalizations pave the way for mediocre teams that severely compromise project success. The hard truth acknowledges no substitutes for A-Player teams on mission-critical initiatives and leaders must take a long view towards talent planning that proactively fosters deep benches.

World-class leaders obsessed with talent management and project excellence reject compromises that surreptitiously doom endeavors from the start. They willingly have courageous conversations, negotiate resourcing agreements far in advance and create talent pipelines supporting strategic initiatives above all else.

By expending political capital to recruit and retain A-Player teams, leaders gift projects the best possibility of driving breakthrough outcomes through the coming challenges that inevitably emerge. With strong teams formed, organizations can then implement governance supporting strategic decision-making.

Establishing Clear Governance & Controls

Finally, running complex projects demands leaders implement clear governance protocols enabling discipline and transparency organization-wide. Much like expert navigators, skilled governance helps teams continually reorient efforts amidst dynamic environments replete with stormy weather, shifting currents and obscured shoals.

Effective governance empowers teams through efficient information flows, decision escalation and resource allocation. Core elements include consistent communications via standardized reports, scheduled reviews aligned to milestones and unambiguous decision rights. For example, leads may retain autonomy around key topics while executives weigh in on strategic rulings involving budgets or major tradeoffs. Together, these controls enable teams to smoothly execute initiatives.

Conversely, gaps introduce friction that rapidly bogs projects down in double work, debates and delays ultimately hindering outcomes. Leaders often overlook governance if previous initiatives proceeded relatively smoothly, however this remains a risky oversight.

In complex endeavors, unforeseen challenges trigger uncertainty that easily overwhelms teams absent governance guardrails to guide next steps. Staff burn endless cycles struggling to realign and regain momentum in the darkness. Only consistent governance protocols provide the structure for teams to systematically work through emerging issues.

Through early establishment of governance schemas, leaders gift teams the strategic processes that ultimately shepherd projects safely through rocky seas towards final destinations. With governance in place, organizations stand ready to translate plans into reality by activating teams towards purposeful action.

Tradeoffs Between Scope, Timeline, and Resources

The enduring success of any project depends on effectively balancing three critical dimensions known as the Iron Triangle: scope, timeline, and cost. Mastery over this framework allows project managers to adaptably guide teams over unpredictable terrain to reach desired destinations. However, mismanaging any one aspect risks collapsing the entire endeavor.

What Makes These Elements So Challenging to Balance?

Individually, scope, timeline, and resources appear straightforward enough. Scope represents the contract of all features and functionality to be delivered. Time describes the expected development duration from kickoff to launch. Resources consist of the labor, budget and materials expended towards execution.

Deceptively simple in isolation, intricate complexities emerge attempting to balance interrelated components. The underlying constraint exists through limited resources available, thus increasing scope and accelerating timelines require greater funding for additional headcount. Yet budgets remain fixed so that scope tradeoffs enable faster delivery. More resources reciprocally drive innovations in scope.

Essentially, expanding any one dimension necessitates concessions across the others to maintain equilibrium. If not carefully controlled, even small imbalances accumulate over time to unleash existential impacts. Delayed timelines sink go-live dates and drain budget reserves. Feature creep explodes functionality outside initial scope banning products to perpetual unreadiness. The balancing act challenges even masters in project leadership.

Environmental Turbulence Compounds Matters

Dynamic business conditions further complicate matters through unpredictable events introducing turmoil. Requirements evolve as customers clarify needs and new ideas emerge. Funding gets curtailed by budget cuts or reappropriated to higher priority projects. Staff bandwidth shrinks under organizational changes prompting turnover.

Navigating disruptions tests a leader's capabilities under pressure to uphold commitments despite uncontrolled forces trying to pull projects dangerously off balance. However, the integrative nature of scope, resources and timeline also presents built-in stabilization points if appropriately utilized.

The seasoned leader remains constantly tuned into the environment to sense shifting dynamics well ahead of visibility. Rather than reacting defensively, proactive stances revisit tradeoff decisions across the Triangle to absorb changes smoothly while protecting overall equilibrium and forward progress. Leaders promote transparent conversations around alterations, setting expectations and rebuilding agreements to bring stakeholders together on updated plans.

Let us explore each point of the Triangle more deeply to reveal interplays and leadership strategies for balance against turbulence.

Defining Project Scope

Project scope captures all the intended deliverables, features, and functionality to be provided through initiatives. Well-defined specifications set expectations around final products built, capabilities offered, performance benchmarks and quality standards. Scope foundations early in initiation enable bid solicitation and planning to happen upstream while downstream developers rely on documentation to craft roadmaps and resource requirements.

However clear initially, scope often remains slippery in practice. Stakeholders submit change requests to satisfy evolving needs or as they envisage previously undescribed opportunities. Leaders often overlook impact assessments to accommodate requests hoping to increase customer satisfaction. However, cumulative changes inflate objectives downstream without adjusting resources or timelines to compensate. Before long, projects find themselves overscoped with no way to deliver.

The Minimum Viable Product Framework

Seasoned leaders lean on Minimum Viable Product (MVP) frameworks to align stakeholder expectations when balancing scope. MVP offers complete, production-ready core functionality addressing the riskiest assumptions around customer needs and product direction. Supplementary capabilities get prioritized into backlogs and delivered through successive iterations beyond launch.

Rather than overinvesting ahead of validation, MVP injects learning cycles that confirm product-solution fits before committing further. Demonstrable releases gather real-world feedback for leaders to assess whether more scope represents the highest ROI. Objective data better informs tradeoff decisions across the Triangle.

Overall, MVPs create maneuverability against turbulence allowing leaders to shape scope based on learning rather than unchecked speculation or pressure. Iteration replenishments resourcefully expand capabilities without overextending projects or teams.

Managing Project Timelines

Project timelines establish expected development cycles from kickoff through deployment with reasonable buffer allocations. However, leaders often struggle estimating durations accurately across long horizons given limited visibility into the amount of effort activities require. Unexpected obstacles likewise emerge turning best case schedules into fantasy.

Agile frameworks address uncertainty introducing short fixed length iterations called sprints which deliver incremental value. Timeboxes scope work into capacity-driven buckets to pull realistic objectives continually. Risks decompose into smaller pieces tackled serially allowing adaptation around emerging conditions. Transparency nurtures collaboration acrossowners to meet recurrent deadlines.

Learning Velocities Anchor Estimates

After several iteration cycles, teams establish reliable velocity metrics measuring story points completed per sprint. Velocities determine backlog volumes teams confidently deliver within bounded timeboxes. Leaders apply sustained output rates to benchmark realistic release targets across projects, balancing available months and staff. Committing beyond validated rates risks severe delays or degradation without proportionate concessions in budget or functionality.

Vigilant Monitoring

While velocities ground long-term planning, leaders also monitor emergent activity daily. Standups socialize impediments needing escalation while burndown charts highlight completions vs workload remaining. Leaders revisit sprint commitments midflight where unforeseen blockers slow completions before timeline concessions get granted. They also protect team health by firmly resisting overburdening individuals with crisis workloads that guarantee future attrition and expertise loss.

Adaptive leaders tap offsets across the Triangle intentionally absorbing some delays overripe for scope reduction or resource enhancement. However, when time truly proves the critical path, transparent tradeoff conversations realign dependencies before trouble cascades irrecoverably.

Optimizing Project Resources

The resource component within the Iron Triangle captures all monetary, human and operational investments devoted to project delivery. Ledgers tally direct funding covering technology, facilities and gear alongside team member payroll. However standardized rates overlooking work complexity, role distributions and utilization inefficiencies distort projections. Hidden delays likewise drain budgets without progress.

Bottom up activity outlines counter superficial budgets with detailed assignments itemizing realistic workload down to hour increments per task. Accuracy improves further incorporating historical project performance benchmarks for activities given team composition and work styles. Leadership openly reviews bottoms up projections fostering ownership for estimates and commitments among delivery owners.

Governance around approvals introduced after initial budgeting ensures tight oversight on spend during execution. Invoice and staffing reviews may cover daily rates and team sizes against targets. Forecasting updates help leadership evaluate progress-to-plan tradeoffs evaluating necessity for out of cycle resource requests.

Leaders maintain affordability balancing project investments and organizational value delivered through rigor and cross functional partnership. However, underspending risks turn into false economies where stretches for savings yield defocused staff and inadequate capabilities unable to sustain output velocities long run.

Adaptive Resourcing

Similar to adjusting timelines, leaders work with finance partners to match resourcing levels to evolving demand signals from scope and pace. Staff grows and contracts across initiative phases per plan avoiding Fri layoffs that sabotage team continuity or emergency contractor piles that maze onboarding. Tools and technology likewise scale appropriately against validated adoption preventing shelfware.

Overall fiscal responsibility ensures projects operate within economical means while still receiving adequate nurturing to thrive. Achieving balance requires financial acumen paired with delivery domain expertise to determine appropriate thresholds. However, partnerships built on transparency and accountability ultimately enable decisions optimizing for the whole, not just narrow portions.

The Iron Triangle of scope, timeline and resources establishes foundational framework for leaders to evaluate and guide project delivery. However, complex interplays between dimensions require constant assessment and balancing to maintain equilibrium and progress. Unknowns and change inject turbulence that easily tips endeavors into disarray absent experienced hands creatively leveraging built-in flexibilities.

Adaptive leaders develop key skill sets including systems thinking, advanced planning, progress monitoring and cross functional collaboration to steer around disruption. Rather than rigidly adhering to plans, they remain responsively aligned to signals from the Triangle itself - adjusting elements in turn to uphold commitments to customers and teams alike. Scope offers some buffer while time and resources pick up slack. Tradeoffs happen intentionally, backed by data.

By mastering navigation across key constraints, leaders uphold project stability and momentum in the face of adversity. They choose the wisest paths harnessing elements already present rather than exerting unsustainable extraordinary effort. In the end, balance sustains the journey.

Strategic Delegation in Project Management

Delegation empowers leaders to accomplish greater goals by distributing work across capable teams. However, simply doling out tasks fails to unleash full potential. Done strategically, delegation serves multiple purposes beyond relieving the manager's burden.

Delegation assigns specific responsibilities to team members best suited for the job based on skills, bandwidth and interests. Rather than hoarding work to prove one's worth or meet personal standards, delegation shares ownership of outcomes across empowered, aligned players.

Beyond task lists, delegation occurs whenever leaders staff project plans, assign action items after meetings or allocate risks to owners. By matching work to strengths, strategic delegation enables higher quality and faster results compared to centralized attempts.

However, many leaders new to management struggle trusting others to produce satisfactory work, fearing lost control or perceptions of being dispensable if no longer doing everything. In reality, little gets accomplished through solo efforts and disengaged teams unlikely step up absent opportunities.

In fact, thoughtful delegation earns deep loyalty by showing genuine care towards direct reports through developing skills, unlocking potential and granting visible impact. Leaders level up their teams to drive shared wins using delegation building trust and influence for future change initiatives.

Consider Delegation an Important Management Skill

Seasoned leaders view delegation as a core management competency on par with strategy, finance or communications. Perfecting delegation directly enables wider organizational influence through compounding returns on time invested into others.

When first delegating to newer team members, start small with tightly scoped tasks squarely in the person's comfort zone before raising degrees of difficulty. Leaders set follow ups to monitor work quality and provide coaching to support growth.

Over time, leaders increasingly challenge trusted players with more complex assignments or leadership opportunities, cementing delegation relationships. However, leaders avoid overburdening high performers at the expense of health or core duties.

Follow the SMARTER Framework

Well-designed delegations clearly communicate desired outcomes and parameters following the SMARTER framework:

Specific: Define the precise objective, requirements and quality expectations. Remove any ambiguity.

Measurable: Establish evaluation criteria and Key Performance Indicators to track progress.

Agreed: Secure commitment demonstrating the team member accepts the responsibility.

Realistic: Validate workloads appropriately fit within scope of skills, available effort and access to resources.

Time-Bound: Provide clear deadlines or durations expected to complete work.

Ethical: Ensure delegated tasks align to team member's values and health boundaries.

Recorded: Document delegations detailing assignments, owners and statuses providing referenceable confirmation.

Check In Frequently

Great execution requires leaders regularly check in on progress across the lifecycle. Early trouble signs provide alerts to quickly clarify any confusion before small issues multiply downstream.

Leaders openly discuss challenges during reviews to determine appropriate support whether through mentoring, more resources or negotiating adjusted timelines. Ultimately both parties share accountability towards finding resolutions.

Beyond the tactical playbook, excellent delegation also requires a growth mindset from leaders seeking to develop team capabilities rather than just extract results.

Tracking and Controlling Project Trajectory

Even flawless plans fail absent vigorous oversight ensuring ideas transform into reality. Monitoring and controlling project progress serves as the essential bridge between thoughtful strategy and capable execution. Rather than crossing fingers that tasks magically align, leaders implement robust tracking frameworks to surface risks early while also guiding teams dynamically towards success.

What is Project Monitoring and Control?

Project monitoring continuously gathers key performance indicators across team efforts, resources, budgets and milestones to evaluate progress against initial plans. Measurements inform control activities adjusting direction or intensity around blocks preventing target achievement.

For example, leaders may redistribute labor or funds to accelerate latestage workstreams while also descoping low value features no longer viable within constraints. Cutting losses counters stubborn persistence when environments or priorities shift mid-flight. Objective data inputs from monitoring allow for decisive, aligned steering.

Together, vigilant tracking and timely interventions keep projects on trajectory to deliver intended outcomes without preventable escalations that ultimately erode value. However, neglecting control procedures is equivalent to sailing onward blindly amidst surging storm waves hoping no treacherous rocks lie ahead. No successful journey unfolds solely on hope alone.

Essential Process Components

Project leaders optimize monitoring and control through implementing seven essential components:

1. Requirements Baseline

2. Schedule Baseline

3. Cost and Resource Plan

4. Risk Register

5. Change Log

6. Quality Assurance Controls

7. Integrated Tracking Tools

Let us explore how each element synergistically creates an early warning and response infrastructure enabling teams to reliably meet commitments despite inevitable turbulence.

Requirements Baseline

The requirements baseline comprehensively documents project scope across all features, functions, outputs and quality standards per original agreements with stakeholders. As shifting demands trigger endless scope creep jeopardizing timely delivery, leaders reference baselines reminding all players what currently remains in or out of bounds per current commitments. Deviations undergo change control processes to renegotiate adjusted terms across the board. An outdated baseline obscures vision, whereas an actively maintained baseline makes progress objectively clear.

Schedule Baseline

In addition to specifying the "what" around project expectations, leaders further construct schedule baselines detailing the "when" for stakeholders via major milestones. Initial roadmaps outline phased task durations, sequences and resource allocations forecasting hand offs across interdependent workstreams. Once signed-off by sponsors, baselines represent fixed contracts allowing leaders to chart actual results against plans transparently demonstrating on-target or slipping progress requiring intervention.

Cost and Resource Plan

Beyond chronicling expected time investments, leaders additionally estimate financial outlays for gear, services and payroll ultimately required realizing deliverables. Bottom-up outlines gather task-level projections from owners most familiar with work complexity, historical data and team bandwidth. Rigorous upfront budgeting uncovers unrealistic expectations early, prompting leaders to revert scope or resources to align executive signoff preventing midstream shortfalls triggering mass descopes. Continual cost forecasting highlights overruns for timely course correction targeting non-mandatory expenditures first before scope reductions upend carefully crafted experiences.

Risk Register

Even anticipating projects based on thoughtful assumptions, unknown factors still emerge disrupting best laid plans. To get ahead of surprises before inflicting disaster, leaders maintain risk registers actively tracking and prioritizing possible scenarios including probabilities and impacts if indeed encountered. Preventative actions outline mitigations to contain threats or exploit opportunities should conditions shift either direction. Reviews during recurring team meetings allow real-time adjustments guiding responses to current issues and insights. Being perpetually vigilant ultimately differentiates proactivity versus reactivity.

Change Log

Despite starting initiatives grounded in essential baselines and risk awareness, new complexities still arise requiring teams to adapt approaches while upholding broader goals. Change logs provide critical repositories formally documenting realignments to schedule, resources and requirements as situations evolve upstream. Timestamped records chronicle when, how and why alterations occurred for future reference. This protects against undue scope creep by confirming deliberate concessions across stakeholders per governance procedures. Logs also notify downstream teams to expected adjustments in their work per open communications.

Quality Assurance Controls

While monitoring scope, cost and velocity remains imperative, leaders additionally implement rigorous quality checks validating that deliverables sufficiently fulfill end user needs at each milestone. Reviews assess functionality, usability and longevity against documented specifications established early on. Test cases replicate diverse real-world scenarios to confirm designs withstand present demands with extendability accommodating foreseeable future needs. Proactive quality frameworks embed user feedback iteratively while defects remain less expensive to remedy upstream rather than upon final service delivery or system deployment. Leadership attention towards consistent quality assurance governs project outcomes.

Integrated Tracking Tools

Finally, fluctuating variables across large-scale initiatives easily overwhelm siloed teams lacking visibility into interconnected impacts beyond narrow assignments. Leaders provide centralized dashboards consolidating indicators from schedules, budgets and requirements into shareable formats promotes transparency. Automated notifications trigger when thresholds hit inflection points requiring intervention based on role. Tools enable nuanced Drilldowns to facilitate root cause analysis while allowing scenarios planning to game decisions. Integrated data fuels efficient steering.

Legendary IT pioneer Tom DeMarco once noted that "you cannot control what you do not measure." For project managers, no truer words get spoken. While initiating efforts brims with optimism and purpose, seasoned veterans acknowledge that plans get battered amidst messy realities.

Rather than crossed fingers, responsive leaders implement robust monitoring operations alongside decisive control mechanisms to track progress, identify variances and guide teams adaptively towards desired targets. Early warning systems trigger proactive course corrections steering around hazards enroute to collective wins while avoiding 11th hour heroics that signify far deeper leadership failures in vigilance. Great plans only endure through great stewardship ensuring vision translates into reality.

Key Takeaways and Final Thoughts on Strategic Project Leadership

Key Takeaways:

- Strategic project leaders focus on laying strong foundations across people, processes, and priorities at the start by clarifying purpose, securing sponsors, assembling A-player teams, and establishing governance. This upfront investment sets initiatives up for success.

- Leading complex initiatives requires vigilantly monitoring variables like scope, budgets, timelines and risks to surface roadblocks early. Adaptive corrective actions keep teams on trajectory through turbulence.

- Empowering teams through thoughtful delegation matching assignments to strengths unlocks greater speed and quality than individual efforts alone. It also develops talent and relationships vital for driving change.

- Overcommunicating with transparency, tailoring, and partnership builds trust and alignment across diverse stakeholders essential for bringing initiatives successfully to fruition.

Mastering Project Leadership

Successfully steering projects from ideas to impact relies as much on leadership art as technical science. While diligent planning and process aptly collates the tangible - tasks, budgets, models - realizing strategic goals ultimately interweaves messy human dynamics. An eye for nuance and connection channels plans into reality.

Seasoned leaders acknowledge people as the locus of success powering endeavors forward through skilled execution or inertia impeding progress. Aligning priorities, surfacing blindspots, dismantling barriers and adapting approaches transforms team potential into kinetic energy accelerating organizations ahead.

Technical mastery alone fails to catalyze movement. Leaders must win hearts and minds securing buy-in across stakeholders through resonance and relationship building. Transparent communications clarifying purpose and progress breeds trust to elevate collaboration. Hands-on mentoring unlocks individual growth accelerating capabilities organization-wide.

Adaptive leaders also remain vigilant to signals from plans and teams alike, steering dynamically towards milestones. They celebrate small early wins establishing momentum while also addressing setbacks directly to restore confidence. By balancing rigor with empathy, they realize greater collective potential.

The fruits of initiatives are only as strong as the streams feeding efforts. Sowing seeds for success requires patient leadership beyond surface level milestones. Though arduous, envisioning projects holistically best equips organizations to seize opportunities ahead. What conversations should leaders enter today to uplift capabilities for tomorrow?

Chapter Six

Setting Goals Strategically

Goal-setting is a near universal leadership practice aimed at driving performance, providing direction, and catalyzing innovation. However, in dynamic work environments characterized by ambiguous objectives, variable workflows, and diverse skill sets, defining suitable goals poses a significant challenge. How then, can managers establish markers for success that balance ambition and achievability? This essay defines strategic goal-setting as a core leadership framework, summarizes prevalent theoretical models and their limitations, analyzes inherent difficulties in modern organizational contexts, and provides research-based recommendations for implementation.

Common Goal-Setting Approaches

The most ubiquitous goal-setting model is the SMART framework, first proposed in a 1981 paper in Management Review by George Doran. As an acronym, SMART denotes that targets should be:

- Specific

- Measurable

- Achievable

- Relevant

- Time-bound

The principle is intuitively sensible - leaders should outline goals that are clearly articulated, quantifiable where possible, moderately difficult but feasible, aligned to priorities, and containing appropriate pacing.

However, empirical investigations reveal notable deficiencies in the SMART goal paradigm. A 2018 study analyzing decades of organizational research literature found that while goal specificity demonstrates some positive effects in simple or routine tasks, evidence does not support the notion that highly specific goals reliably enhance performance. In complex tasks involving creativity, relationship-building, or cross-functional collaboration, rigid prescriptions actually constrained productive behaviors. Furthermore, the study found no basis for the model's core premise that moderately difficult goals optimize motivation and effort.

Additional studies have called into question the effectiveness of SMART goal dimensionality altogether. A 2015 paper investigated how leadership attributes interacted with goal parameters in shaping performance. Results showed that factors like goal orientation, optimism, and vision orientation were far more predictive of superior outcomes than properties of the goals themselves. This suggests organizational leaders play a pivotal role in contextualizing and communicating goals to catalyze motivation.

Problems with Realistic Goal-Setting

When faced with uncertainty regarding optimal goal difficulty, many leaders default to setting seemingly "realistic" objectives deemed cautiously achievable. This approach aligns to broader management philosophies grounded in scientific rationalism and reasonableness. However, data reveals consistent underestimation of actual team capabilities and the pace of potential progress when goals err conservative.

A 2019 empirical study compiled decades of field research on the relationship between goal difficulty and team performance. Findings demonstrated unambiguously that more difficult goals produced substantially higher performance levels compared to lenient targets. Easy goals failed to stimulate critical evaluation, collective learning, or concerted effort. Teams with clear visions for breakthrough outcomes developed new capabilities and tools to expand conceived possibility.

Researchers proposed explanations centered on social cognition and motivation. Ambitious markers tap into deeper shared purpose and meaning while precipitating higher situational awareness, information exchange, and coordination. Progress feels energizing. Setbacks prompt iteration rather than resignation. By contrast, easy goals foster complacency and activate biases clouding objective assessment.

While proponents argue moderately difficult goals demonstrate considerate leadership, teamsactually achieve exponentially more over time when framed challenges compel members to re-conceive their potential. Leaders must therefore set aside simplistic notions of realism when setting strategic goals.

KPIs vs. OKRs

As a leader, setting clear goals and tracking progress is essential to realizing your vision and empowering teams. However, with countless frameworks and methodologies touted as silver bullets, navigating options proves daunting. Here, we examine two prominent goal setting approaches – key performance indicators (KPIs) and objectives and key results (OKRs). We'll overview origins and definitions, comparative strengths and weaknesses, primary applications, and recommendations for integrated deployment to amplify impact.

KPIs Defined

First introduced by ministers measuring performance in the Wei Dynasty centuries ago, key performance indicators (KPIs) are metrics gauging progress towards predefined targets.

For example, ecommerce managers commonly set KPIs for metrics like average order value, customer lifetime value, and conversion percentages. By setting specific quantifiable markers then tracking trends, leaders understand market reception, emerging needs and resource efficacy.

KPIs embody simple questions:

- Is this working?

- Are we headed in the right direction?

If a KPI drops below an acceptable threshold, leaders investigate underlying causes through drill-down analyses or supplemental inquiries. Falling short of a sales target might prompt customer surveys, website analytics, interviewing staff about pain points or checking for market disruptions.

By distilling complex processes into numerical outputs and monitoring frequently, KPIs enable evidence-based corrections keeping initiatives on course.

Selecting KPIs

Effective KPIs share several traits:

- *Quantifiable:* KPIs represent measurable values like revenue, cost, churn rate and customer satisfaction scores. Qualities like "good teamwork" prove difficult to track reliably.

- *Relevant:* KPIs directly gauge progress toward goals meaningful for success. Tracking social media followers matters less for a b2b startup than call answer rates.

- *Timely:* Frequent measurement enables rapid response. Monthly metrics catch issues faster than annual reviews.

- *Reliable:* KPIs should have consistent, well-defined calculation methods unaffected by subjective judgment.

Once identified, plot historical data to determine acceptable thresholds and feasible target growth. If website clicks plateaued at 100 daily for the past year, suddenly driving 300 overnight seems improbable without significant changes. Set realistic goals by examining what's worked previously.

KPI Use Cases

Since KPIs quantify progress on existing goals, they best suit repeatable processes around traction, efficiency and scale. Common applications include:

- Marketing: MQLs, cost per lead, turnover rates

- Sales: Win rates, average deal sizes

- Support: Ticket resolution times, satisfaction

- Product: Active users, adoption metrics

- Project Management: Budget versus actual spend

By continuously inspecting key numbers, teams maintain alignment while catching deviations early. Each metric acts like a compass towards the north star vision.

However, KPIs merely represent outputs. The approach lacks mechanisms for deciding optimal goals or questioning underlying assumptions. KPIs quantify rather than qualify efforts.

Section 2: Objectives and Key Results (OKRs)

OKRs Defined

Pioneered by Intel then popularized by Google, objectives and key results (OKRs) are goals denoting measurable milestones for an ambitious target. Objectives reflect qualitative aims while key results are quantitative signifiers of progress.

For example, an engineering manager might create the following objective and key results:

Objective: Launch AI-powered support bots

Key Result 1: Complete building contextual dialogue system by December
Key Result 2: Achieve 80% bot accuracy on sample conversations by January
Key Result 3: Ensure 95% availability for first month post-release

Leaders establish objectives, teams suggest key results, and regular reflection fuels learning. OKRs distill lofty aspirations into actionable stepping stones tuned as efforts unfold.

John Doerr, former Intel exec and OKR proponent, declared the approach "a management methodology that helps to ensure employees work together towards the same goals". Alignment stems from collaborative formulation and centralized tracking.

OKR Qualities

Effective OKR setting requires thoughtfully constructed objectives meeting several criteria:

- *Ambitious:* OKRs should seem slightly out of reach, not like default yearly targets. Reaching for 10% growth when 50% feels possible signals undershooting potential.

- *Qualitative:* Objectives capture the essence of what's sought. Consider "launch industry-leading customer portal" rather than "increase site clicks".

- *Inspirational:* Align objectives to core values and purpose. Focus on the why before determining key results.

- *Time-bound:* Quarterly OKRs fuel urgency while allowing last minute goal posts changes if learning reveals unforeseen challenges.

Leaders shouldn't expect 100% of OKRs to hit green each cycle. Google famously notes that if all OKRs show as accomplished, teams aren't thinking big enough! The process centers on aligned effort and innovation, not flawless execution.

OKR Use Cases

With emphasis on conceptual objectives plus quantitative tracking, OKRs best facilitate:

- Mission-critical goals around products, programs or business lines

- Top-level alignment across departments

- Innovation outside core operations

Rather than minutely inspecting existing metrics like KPIs, OKRs provide structured blueprints for manifesting visions. They operationalize strategy.

Consequently, OKRs inject clarity amid business transformations by defining essential milestones inevitable in retrospect but utterly unforeseeable at outset. They rally people around not why execution matters right now but where collective potential can take them next.

Key Differences and Integration Opportunities

While KPIs and OKRs both quantify targets central to strategy, several inherent differences determine suitability:

- KPIs track ongoing metrics; OKRs outline milestone markers

- KPIs monitor; OKRs lead

- KPIs gauge efficiency; OKRs drive ambitious innovation

Distinct applications become apparent:

KPIs: Where are we right now regarding x? How can we improve?
OKRs: Where do we aim to reach by y date? What must we architect to manifest that future?

However, integrating approaches unlocks immense value:

- KPIs supply baselines for orienting OKRs. Quarterly sales averaged $50 000? An ambitious objective might target $250 000 through revised positioning.

- OKRs explain KPI fluctuations. Spiking customer churn likely traces to that risky platform migration initiation. Retention OKRs now receive priority.

This interplay enables data-informed ambition. KPIs ground lofty OKRs in reality checks while the reverse makes lagging KPIs actionable. Together they facilitate timely course correction.

Leaders overlooking objective data in pursuit of gut-feel breakthroughs often underperform more balanced peers. Coupling metrics into a navigation system helps prevent teams losing sight of true north.

With KPIs evaluating ongoing effectiveness and OKRs driving purposeful expansion, integrated deployment allows organizations to extend reach ambitiously without compromising stability. The symbiotic framework fulfils growing complexity at scale.

A Leader's Guide to Setting Goals with KPIs and OKRs

Hopefully you now grasp distinctions within the goal setting landscape and recognize opportunities for blended approaches. Here I provide recommendations for rolling out KPI and OKR systems.

Getting Started

As Peter Drucker famously declared, "What's measured improves." If goal setting remains vague, execution inevitably follows suit. Begin reviewing operations through an optimization lens.

- What key numbers currently guide planning?

- Which statistics would indicate growth?

Flip between bird's eye questions assessing overall ecosystem health and worm's eye investigations drilling into nuances behind trends. Gradually product, project and process KPIs will emerge.

Similarly, ask department heads for wild visions if limitations disappeared. Push teams to formulate objectives for disruptive innovation. Debate merits until inspirational OKRs crystallizing advancement appear.

Carefully Separate Metrics

KPIs and OKRs serve complementary yet distinct purposes. Confusion severely hampers effectiveness for both. Routinely classify targets using simple frameworks:

KPI: Input metrics tracking key operations
OKR: Milestone markers of ambitious initiatives

Leaders often assign OKRs then demand KPI-like tracking. However, if an objective centers on building capabilities to enter new markets, pedantic quantified monitoring proves counterproductive. Focus on engagements, learnings and barriers. Save precise KPIs for new efficiencies in existing arenas.

Create Tracking Systems

With goals defined, establishment centralized systems allows easy input and access for stakeholders company-wide. Many project management softwares like Asana or AirTable allow custom tracking. Well-designed interfaces prominently showcase KPIs and OKRs while allowing drill-down for details like historical performance and goal setting methodologies.

Make reporting, reviewing and revising regular routines. Schedule monthly OKR progress checks between managers and direct reports. Review KPIs across broader teams quarterly.

Transparent tracking builds collective ownership for outcomes while surfacing creative strategies from unexpected contributors.

Aligning Team Goals with Organizational Strategy

Creating alignment between team objectives and overarching organizational strategy is foundational for unlocking potential, accelerating growth and empowering people. However, with limited guidance on practical integration, leaders often struggle upholding strategy as teams tackle daily demands. This section provides an actionable framework for interweaving goals across company levels to catalyze focus and engagement.

The Value of Connected Goals

Research conclusively demonstrates strategic alignment, whereby employees view personal goals as intrinsically linked to company mission, substantially boosts performance. Groups experiencing unity of purpose achieve more in less time with greater job satisfaction.

However, despite advantages, only 40% of staff across surveyed enterprises can accurately name organizational goals. Workplace disengagement traces directly to perceived irrelevance.

By actively tying lower-level goals to overarching corporate strategy, leaders both streamline efforts and reengage talent. The following steps create cascading objectives unifying teams.

Top-Level Goal Setting

Hierarchy matters when aligning teams. Organizational objectives form the foundation determining initiative prioritization, resource allocation and progress benchmarks.

Leadership must firstly clarify corporate goals based on vision and values. If espousing bold innovation, set stretch targets for internal capabilities development, product upgrades and market expansion. Use quarterly OKRs to maintain ambition.

Equally importantly, repeatedly communicate chosen goals across management channels. Discuss in meetings, host summits, circulate newsletters and embed in reviews. With priorities transparent, mid-level leaders will integrate direction into their domains.

Driving Middle Manager Buy-In

With corporate goals defined, directors must contextualize for their divisions. Finance translates targets into budget scenarios while Marketing develops promotional campaigns.

Host collaborative sessions allowing managers to review leadership aims then formulate supportive objectives. Rather than handed-down directives, facilitate creative empowerment leveraging insider expertise. Voice demonstrates value.

Address doubts transparently by connecting choices to growth, satisfaction and sustainability. Evolved priorities then gain champions across organizations, not arbitrary edicts. Patient exchange cements loyalty to collective advancement.

Empowering Employee Goal Ownership

Finally, frontline staff REQUIRE exposure to the why underpinning company purpose before fully engaging individual goal setting.

How can teams commit to niche targets without grasping overarching vision? Tactically, leaders from the top down must reference aligned objectives when assigning tasks. For example, "This networking gives work deeper meaning which researching software requirements to enter China" resonates more profoundly by helping team members understand market expansion underpins a unifying sales goal.

With context given, managers should encourage employees ideating personal objectives supporting established organizational goals. Regular check-ins fuel iterative refinement to maximize business and professional returns simultaneously.

By naming shared vision, strategically aligning management imperatives and helping individuals locate purpose in corporate aims, organizations gain incredible power to enact transformative agendas. 37signals CEO Jason Fried noted that "Goal alignment helps companies carry out sophisticated projects with little formal oversight." The integrated approach works when all contributors own a piece of the whole.

Tracking Progress and Adjusting Goals

Goal setting represents a starting line. Tracking and adaptation pave the path to realization. Through progress inspection, teams identity what propels them forwards and what holds them back. Leaders able to dynamically steer groups based on emergent obstacles and opportunities ultimately reach destinations quicker.

This comprehensive guide examines goal tracking fundamentals, highlighting best practices for review and revision cycles. We'll cover breaking down sizable objectives, assigning realistic timelines, monitoring collective advancement and recalibrating efforts when necessary. With insights into the metrics, meetings and mindsets underpinning achievement, you'll lead teams adept adapting efforts today to manifest ambitious visions tomorrow.

Granular Goal Setting

In 1883, Italian economist Vilfredo Pareto noted that approximately 80% of consequences flow from 20% of causes. This 80/20 principle proves especially relevant when managing complex projects. Research shows that by prioritizing key elements with outsized impact we accomplish more in less time.

The ethos applies directly to lofty corporate goals involving lengthy development hurdles before realization. Rather than tracking messy abstractions, leaders should break down sizable targets into incremental mile markers built upon SMART methodology.

For example, consider a startup aiming to develop artificial intelligence healthcare chatbots. The following incremental OKRs better track progress:

Key Result 1 - Complete contextual dialogue system fundamentals
Key Result 2 – Chatbots accurately respond to 80% of sample patient conversations
Key Result 3 – Ensure minimum 95% uptime during initial hospital trial

With incremental stepping stones marked, teams traverse seeming unscalable ascents one measured stride at a time. Progress flows from small wins accumulating, not quantum leaps suddenly materializing.

Smart Deadline Setting

Just as essential as decomposing monumental goals is constructing associated realistic timelines to coordinate efforts. Leaders must critically examine each objective, consult specialists and historical benchmarks then assign ambitious but achievable due dates.

While padding estimates buffers unforeseen delays, research shows improbable deadlines actually catalyze faster results assuming teams buy into targets. The

Death Valley Curve demonstrates that when timelines seem ridiculous initially but purpose resonates, groups discover unseen efficiencies mid-journey.

However, securing commitment requires transparency. Managers should gather input from staff executing tasks and carefully weigh feedback against past performance. Does a developer truly need 3 months for programming or is uncertainty clouding judgment? Discrepancies signal chances for coaching. Still, imposed compression often backfires if teams feel cornered. Inspirational leaders align, they don't mandate.

Overall, carefully calibrate milestones marking the path between today's capabilities and tomorrow's goals. Whether spaced aggression or unreasonable asks, ensure teams believe achievement possible with support.

Consistency in Tracking

With incremental goals plotted across pragmatic horizons, leaders must implement robust tracking to accelerate realization. KPI dashboards centralizing key quantitative metrics and qualitative self-reported progress form objective snapshots for regularly calibration.

Software platforms like Asana, Airtable and Range offer customizable interfaces with interactive visualizations ideal for cross-functional OKR tracking. However, legacy spreadsheet reports or whiteboard updates encourage organic information sharing critical for alignment too.

Core to every approach resides consistency in measurement and transparent distribution to empower action. Set calendar invites for recurring check-ins or make attendance mandatory for meetings. Without rhythmic inspection, the keenest groups lose momentum while others wander aimlessly.

Analysis Over Annotation

Simply archiving scores of static achievement data lacks contextual relevance though. Leaders must dedicate time analyzing trends in cause-effect detail then redirecting accordingly. Why did website conversions suddenly spike last month? How can we spread creative marketing tactics team-wide?

This analytical orientation combats reflexive annotation where managers arbitrarily score progress without considering underlying drivers. You can't affect what you don't inspect at root level. Use tracking to reveal barriers and bright spots equally.

Adapting Support Strategically

Finally, reconfiguring resources and recalibrating goals represent the terminal stage of the tracking lifecycle. Look for emerging needs or overabundances through relative metric performance then address discrepancies to empower smooth flows organizationally.

Does clothing manufacturing require another month before deadline while packaging meets targets early? Realign talent or priorities between divisions to shave lead time. Such nimble role adjustments require relinquishing departmental silos for shared accountability though, so incentivize cooperation.

Leaders as Linkages

Goal tracking and adaptation only enhances performance when functioning as a living system reshaping strategy, not inert artifacts filed away yearly. By regularly zooming out to examine indicator patterns and zooming into breakdown causes for deviations, managers fluidly steer progress.

Yet pacing and course corrections ultimately interlink along a chain of leaders advocating staff needs laterally and upwards. No one individual can address obstacles single-handedly. Transparent tracking maps challenges while manager meetings generate solutions via better integration.

Thus by touring operations, communicating learnings and championing resources redistribution, leaders transform isolated metrics into insights that launch organizations closer toward actualizing once-distant goals.

Decentralizing Tracking

While consistent tracking and responsive direction-setting represent essential leadership tasks, managers shouldn't monopolize all optimization efforts. Research confirms that decentralizing goal monitoring across teams boosts buy-in while uncovering locally optimal workflows.

Empower staff to design creative metrics or review cycles resonating with operational realities on the ground. The marketing manager understands campaign sticking points better than executive leadership largely removed. Provide autonomous space to build helpful systems.

Leaders should additionally encourage peer-to-peer or manager-report goal checking rather than solely relying on top-down reviews. Social accountability activates urgency and camaraderie simultaneously. Public commitment and friendly competition drive achievement too.

Collaborative Reviews

Regular collaborative reviews likewise enhance engagement and illuminate blindspots. Try allocating time during recurring team meetings for members to openly discuss goal progress. Identify struggling points and brainstorm potential solutions.

Managers participate but mostly observe. Healthy debate signals investment while organically airing structural disconnects between expectations and enablement. People want clarity connecting work to collective purpose. Discussion provides visibility.

Additionally, consider occasionally frontloading collaborative reviews before executive status briefings. Let project leaders first talk through adjustments, resources needs and support strategies peer-to-peer before seeking sanctioning. Grassroots governance facilitates speedy iteration.

Incentivizing Alignment

Finally, strategic reward systems maintain teams progressing cooperatively towards growth goals once initial excitement fades. Design recognition programs celebrating milestones achievement at individual, group and organizational tiers.

Public praise for completing foundational tasks encourages those struggling. Smaller prizes like gift cards keep people progressing. Quarterly trips or celebrations for accomplishing primary targets inject fun while actualizing collective purpose.

However, take care incentivizing collaboratively, not competitively to prevent intra-team friction. Foster connection to the mission, not egoistic achievement. With shared dedication secured through equity and inclusion, ambitious visions unfold.

The Power of Project Management Software

Project management software seamlessly centralizes then coordinates the goal setting, tracking and adapting process across organizations. Platforms like Asana, Airtable, Jira and Range enable configurable cascading alignments between individual objectives and overarching organizational goals.

Core features like interactive dashboards, automated reminders, progress visualized through charts and permissions determining access keep everyone energized and informed. Syncingstructures traditionally managedthrough ineffective meetings and endless email chains.

Strength depends enormously on consistent usage standards though. Beforeimplementation, thoughtfully design database schema and interface views with department leaders then train extensively. Revisit and optimize periodically post-launch together.

Employees stay engaged when seeing information flows simplified through technology. Softwares become the digital nervous center transmitting signals between strategic brains directing corporate bodies. Intuitive visibility keeps critical components running smoothly towards ambitious aims.

added value from these platforms emerges from workflow structural transformation, not simply migrating antiquated reports digitally. Thoughtfully reimagine how work integrates across siloed teams and hierarchical levels with software capabilities in mind. What inefficiencies can holistic interfaces solve?

Decode and Customize

Additionally, when evaluating goal tracking softwares, determine which solution best aligns to organizational maturity and workflow needs by decoding industry jargon.

Lightweight tools like Range offer convenient interfaces for engagement tracking and notes aggregation but lack advanced functionality like workload balancing. However, the focused scope enhances user adoption. Alternatively, sophisticated platforms like Asana and Jira enable custom modeling of intricate operational ecosystems yet prove overwhelming initially without diligent optimization.

Ideally, leaders should start simply then scale capabilities as team fluency with foundational features improves. Trying boiling oceans day one drowns everyone in possibilities. Prioritize fundamentals first.

The key insight lies in realizing technology only enhances flows. So before purchasing expensive softwares, honestly assess whether cultural and operational infrastructure exists maximizing utility. Can groups even track goals efficiently without digital aids currently? Start strengthening analog tracking habits before layering software supports.

Think Before You Tech

A final caveat merits mentioning regarding over-indexing technology for engagement. Project management software relies entirely on consistent human usage for entering updates and taking action on insights. Without disciplined inputs, flashy interfaces filled with meaningless scores and outdated accomplishments provide little motivational energy.

Leaders must nurture the cultural soil of accountability, transparency and adaptability enabling technology to blossom. Analog goal setting, reviews and meetings build the

Key Takeaways and Final Thoughts on Setting Goals Strategically

Key Takeaways:

- Leaders must set ambitious stretch goals rooted in organizational purpose and values to compel innovation. Rather than status quo preservation, teams require galvanizing visions of future potential.

- Balance ambition with achievability by scaffolding incremental objectives across pragmatic time horizons. Mark progress through data-driven tracking then recalibrate efforts responsive to emergent needs.

- Cascading alignment between top-level OKRs, department KPIs and individual goals clarifies purpose while granting autonomy for localized optimizations. Establish clear connectivity between efforts.

- Consistent tracking is essential but insufficient alone. Leaders must dedicate recurring time analyzing trends and barriers in depth, then adapt resourcing and goals accordingly rather than just archiving scores.

- Foster collaboration by decentralizing tracking ownership across teams and enabling bottom-up review cycles. Software aids transparency when respecting capability maturity limitations initially. Incentivize milestones.

Strategic Goal Tracking and Adapting

Ambitious goals catalyze innovation yet only through balanced tracking and adaptation do teams ultimately reach finish lines. Rather than fixed mandated milestones, progress unfolds through fluid interactions between data-driven insights, supportive adjustments and participative enthusiasm.

Effective leaders focus less on arbitrary endpoints and more on championing enrichment felt along collective journeys. They celebrate small wins frequently while pivoting strategies responding to emergent obstacles. By maintaining sympathetic orientation towards staff experience, managers rhythmically realign work to resonate with higher purpose.

Trust in human potential proves foundational. With focused direction-setting and progress tracking, groups transcend perceived constraints to reach unprecedented heights aligned to vision. However, even the brightest beacons remain unreachable without first nurturing growth mindsets and supportive cultures empowering teams believing ambitious dreams manifestable.

The question thus becomes, how will you inspire others reaching farther through your leadership today? What bold possibility might we address jointly tomorrow?

Chapter Seven

Financial Acumen for Leaders

L eadership today demands far more than charisma and vision; it requires the ability to guide organizations through complexity and uncertainty with strategic foresight. And in our data-driven world, financial literacy provides an invaluable context for decision-making that separates thriving leaders from the rest. Yet finance remains an intimidating domain for many - akin to learning a foreign language. This need not be the case. With some dedicated effort to decode the grammar of money and numbers, anyone can develop the financial fluency necessary to speak this universal language of business.

Demystifying the Building Blocks

The first step to overcoming such intimidation is demystifying core financial concepts and terminology. Consider assets, liabilities, equity, income, expenses, profitability - these form the backbone of financial statements that offer a snapshot of organizational health. Asset refers to anything of material or intangible value owned; liability signals financial obligations; equity captures residual value after settling all debts; income constitutes earnings; expenses denote operational costs and investments; profitability measures the surplus between the two. Contextual clarity on such elementary vocabulary provides initial framing to make sense of financial communications.

Of course, terminology alone offers limited utility without comprehending how these constructs translate to quantitative indicators and trends. Here is where the three essential financial documents come into play - the balance sheet, income statement, and cash flow statement. The balance sheet highlights assets, liabilities, and equity at any given point. The income statement summarizes incomes and expenses over a period. Finally, the cash flow statement depicts inflows and outflows of cash. In tandem, these documents tell a rich story about an organization's financial position and performance trajectory.

Leaders would do well to regularly review such statements, not merely as compliance, but to inform strategic evaluations and planning. Consider investment decisions that promise attractive returns but also increase liability risks that may undermine stability. The balance sheet offers clues on prudent options. Pricing dilemmas to accelerate growth may look different when factoring scalability constraints highlighted in the income statement. Even talent retention issues may take on new meaning when cash flows reveal gaps between forecasting and funding realities for expansion plans used to attract employees. In essence, financials provide indispensable lenses to complement operational insights.

Financial literacy fundamentally enables leaders to bridge the gaps between functions, synthesize disparate ideas, and strategize cohesive game plans for organizations to sustain performance across market volatilities. It provides a means to simplify complexity for coherent decision-making in the face of uncertainty - the hallmarks of strategic leadership. And given finance's positioning as the underlying grammar guiding companies, financial fluency offers a critical lynchpin for management effectiveness.

The domain need not be esoteric either. With consistent immersion in the language that money represents, financial literacy can become second nature. Mastering this language also prevents overreliance on finance teams to always translate the narrative. Instead, leaders develop the acumen to decipher implications themselves and shape the story. So rather than perceive financials as restrictive guidelines, embrace them as launch pads for opportunity. Let numbers show the way so you can strategically lead. Through learning this language, leaders gain an incredible vehicle to guide organizations where words alone cannot. The path to fluency simply starts with curiosity and courage to engage.

The Art of Financial Storytelling

But raw financial data alone fails to elucidate the complete narrative needed for leadership decision-making. This is where financial storytelling comes in - the ability to translate numbers into actions by contextualizing trends and indicators. Skilled financial storytelling involves teasing out key takeaways from volumes of data to identify inflection points, make projections, pinpoint problems, and most importantly, outline solutions.

For instance, a sharp accountant may determine that R&D investments are not yielding patent outputs projected in the initial viability proposal. An adept financial storyteller goes further to outline three reasons for the disconnect, providing alternative formulations for resource allocation across patent categories to optimize returns. In doing so, such a leader bridges silos across functions like R&D, legal, innovation, strategy, and finance to create targeted execution roadmaps. This ability to give voice to financial data is an underappreciated skill that distinguishes strategic leadership.

It entails simplifying complexity without losing rigor and resolution. It means foregrounding material factors while still accounting for uncertainties. Beyond numbers, units, and currencies, financial storytelling infuses vision and purpose. In many ways, it represents translation skills similar to communicating across languages, drawing upon emotional intelligence and intuition rather than pure quantitative reasoning. Leaders must learn to listen to what financials whisper and observe what they do not always divulge outright. Therein lies strategic revelation.

Financial Literacy for Leaders

As a manager, the numbers on financial documents can feel akin to interpreting hieroglyphics. Intimidating columns of figures and head-spinning jargon tend to obscure meaning more than illuminate insight. Yet financial literacy serves as an invaluable skill for managerial decision-making and leadership. Rather than evade financials as esoteric equations, reframe them as a universal language that guides organizations. One simply needs the right decoders to translate data into drivers of motivation, alignment, and goal-setting across teams. With some dedicated effort, managers can develop financial fluency to inform strategy and operations.

Where to Start: Key Financial Documents

Gaining literacy begins with comprehending the three essential financial statements - the balance sheet, income statement, and cash flow statement. Consider these the grammar, vocabulary and narrative structure to make communication with money possible.

The balance sheet highlights assets, liabilities, and equity at a fixed point, providing a health snapshot. Assets, such as cash, inventory, or intellectual property, represent items of value owned. Liabilities signal financial obligations owed. Equity indicates residual ownership value.

The income statement summarizes incomes and expenses over a period, particularly focused on profitability. Incomes constitute earnings from sales, services, or investments. Expenses denote costs for operations, production, salaries and other outlays. The bottomline profit result determines success.

Finally, the cash flow statement depicts inflows and outflows during a timeframe across three categories - operating, investing and financing. Operating cash flows track working capital - earnings less expenses related to core operations. Investing cash flows follow asset-shaping outlays like technology upgrades. Financing cash flows highlight fund raising and repayments.

In unison, these statements narrate a rich financial story to direct strategic decisions. Much like learning vocabulary and grammar before writing essays or reports, managers need foundational fluency here to decode statements into drivers of motivation, alignment and goal-setting across teams.

6 Pathways to Transform Data into Decisive Leadership

Specifically, consider six pathways to convert financial literacy into enhanced decision-making:

1. *Measure impact:* Attribute revenue gains and cost savings to specific projects using income statement data. Analyze which efforts pay off.

2. *Streamline budgets:* Use past financial statements prudently as guides for future budgets, given shifting market landscapes. Focus on high-value investments.

3. *Cut inefficiencies:* Pinpoint redundant tools, services and activities adding limited value from line-item expenses. Redirect savings strategically.

4. *Strategize goals:* Assimilate health snapshots, profitability momentum and capital capacity from cross-linking all statements to define strategic plans.

5. *Foster alignment:* Ensure unified visions across departments by evaluating statements collectively to surface priorities and trade-offs.

6. *Boost motivation:* Showcase employee impact on incomes and highlight how achieving benchmarks outlined in statements create organizational value.

With these steps, financial statements transform from mandatory documents to active guides for decisive leadership. Consider each statement akin to a compass, GPS navigator and fuel indicator for navigating organizations strategically. Only with adept financial map reading skills can managers traverse uncertain market terrains effectively.

Mastering the Basics: A 6-Step Fluency Blueprint

But where to even start cultivating such mastery? Here is a starter roadmap requiring just 15-30 minutes every quarter:

1. *Demystify jargon:* Learn essential financial terms - assets, liabilities, equity, income, expenses, profitability, operating/investing/financing cash flows. Fluency starts small.

2. *Review reports routinely:* Scan statements without getting lost in details. Gradually observe metrics and trends over sequential quarters.

3. *Request relevant extracts:* Ask finance teams to provide simplified reports with metrics aligned to your department's decision needs rather than full statements.

4. *Construct narratives:* Link 2-3 metrics to projects worked on over the last quarter. Describe how they manifested in financial performance using precise vocabulary.

5. *Co-evaluate with colleagues:* Explain observable connections between activities and financial indicators to peers. Invite alternate narratives. Develop collective comprehension.

6. *Impart insights proactively:* Share findings from personal analysis during team meetings, even if not required. Gradually make financial literacy part of organizational culture.

With such micro-steps, managers shift from evading financials to embracing them as enablers of effectiveness and essential decision filters. The learning curve also flattens when managers motivate teams in simplifying statements jointly rather than tackling complexity alone. Within a few quarters, noticing financial patterns, connections and deviations becomes second nature rather than a chore. Numbers transform into an intuitive language for strategy, much like managers learn to scan operational reports or client briefs. But it starts small, with curiosity over apprehension.

With active attempts to better grasp terminology, trends and implications, financial statements transition gradually from intimidating to illuminating. The numbers begin to speak more clearly once managers invest time in building familiarity - they whisper insights, reveal interconnections and guide decisions. Financial literacy serves as the ultimate transferable skill across diverse leadership roles - it fosters alignment, concentrates vision and helps make informed choices amid uncertainty. But cultivating such fluency relies first on managers taking the initiative to nurture understanding and shed avoidance.

The six steps outlined above serve that purpose in offering a low-stakes starting point. Additionally, it helps to view financial statements more as fuels for motivation than restrictive guidelines. Let the numbers show the way forward rather than dictate directions. Money talks louder once managers invest in understanding what it tries saying beyond just digits - it imparts strategy, conveys culture and shapes collective priorities when one learns how to listen. But that starts with managers taking the first steps through the fundamentals. Navigating the financial landscape confidently then becomes far less daunting, much like learning any new language simply requires patience with initial unfamiliarity. Leaders who embrace financial literacy discover incredible vehicles to steer organizations confidently. So start small but start now - translate numbers into narratives and let money reveal its strategic stories. It starts with basic vocabulary but results ultimately in visionary leadership.

Budgeting for Strategic Initiatives

An oft-cited statistic notes that 9 out of 10 organizations fail to execute strategy smoothly. Financial disconnects represent a pivotal reason. Strategies derail when budgets misalign with long-term goals, thereby working at cross-purposes. An effective budget fuels an organization's journey towards strategic targets rather than passively tracking expenses. It directs how each dollar links back to corporate vision. In doing so, a budget evolves from an accounting tool into a planning roadmap for decision-making across departments. Baking strategic alignment into budgeting processes through structured approaches can prove critical for organizations to traverse changing marketplace terrain adeptly.

Where Conventional Budgets Fall Short

Traditionally, annual budgets result from extrapolating previous year spend and adjusting nominal percentages for inflation or operational fluctuations. Department heads negotiate for incremental additions while finance leaders moderate requests to match historical benchmarks for prudence. However, such incremental budgeting suffers inherent limitations.

For one, leadership rarely revisits organizational priorities when applying largely mechanized percentage lifts. Consequently, existing activities receive funding by default without evaluating true strategic value. Critical long-term investments end up starved for funds while outdated programs retain budgets simply from precedent.

Additionally, incremental budgets foster siloed thinking across functions. Departments push to maximize their piece of the pie rather than weighing cross-departmental trade-offs collaboratively. Local optimizations impede organization-wide strategy.

Finally, static budgets fail to account for marketplace uncertainties or seizures of emerging opportunities. They offer little flexibility for course corrections if initial projections deviate due to internal efficiencies or external discontinuities. Financial discipline then discourages growth pursuit.

Although traditional budgets provide prudence and predictability, they often end up working against adaptive execution. So how can organizations embrace long-term strategic vision and prepare for market dynamism simultaneously? Welcome strategic budgeting.

Fusing Strategy with Budgets

Strategic budgeting mechanisms ensure budgets dynamically link back to corporate vision and strategies across planning horizons rather than simply extrapolating previous spend. Leadership first defines long-term objectives considering evolving threats and opportunities. The budgeting process then involves allocating financial resources to key initiatives based on their potential to catalyze these objectives.

For instance, leadership may recognize digital channel expansion as central to future-proofing business models. Consequently, budget proposals from functions like Marketing, eCommerce, Digital Experience and even HR Talent Acquisition would involve technology adoption, cross-team mobilization and capability development. Integrated portfolio views determine optimal resource allocation across such use cases instead of fragmented departmental spend requests.

In doing so, budgets transform from departmental expense sheets to targeted investment portfolios managed like strategic programs. Qualitative evaluation supplements conventional number crunching to fluidly fund priorities. With budgets organically realigned to corporate objectives every cycle, they foster synergy rather than siloed thinking. Leadership also retains flexibility to ramp initiatives up or down based on evolving market insights. Ultimately strategic budgeting serves organizational nimbleness - making resources flow towards the most promising pathways mapped by strategy rather than solely chasing previous years' inertia.

Of course, methodically integrating such budget-strategy fusion has its share of challenges compared to business-as-usual budgeting. It requires financial discipline coupled with growth ambition, centralized oversight alongside contextual input from ground operations and coordinated cross-departmental planning instead of disparate negotiations. But organizations ranging from young startups to industry behemoths have shown how ingraining strategy-aligned budgeting as a leadership muscle can unlock transformational gains. The question simply comes down to commitment rather than capability.

A 4 Step Playbook for Strategic Budgeting

Effectively harnessing budgets to fuel corporate strategy relies on four inter-locked components - vision alignment, opportunity prioritization, portfolio balancing and execution agility.

Step 1: Strategic Alignment

The first step involves revisiting corporate vision considering emerging external discontinuities and internal capability advancements. Leadership must refresh perspectives on market evolution, competitive threats, technological disruptions, operational efficiencies and talent readiness. This allows taking a clean slate view to determine priorities rather than perpetuating legacy programs just because they secured past funding.

Step 2: Opportunity Prioritization

With an updated strategic vision, identify signature initiatives that can catalyze progress by capitalizing on emergent opportunities or countering risk exposures. Avoid constraining creativity too early but also prevent laundry listing every possible activity. Sharp prioritization enables separating high potential accelerators from marginal improvements. Structure selection criteria to smoothly fund down funnel initiatives once proof of viability surfaces from early stage experimentation.

Step 3: Portfolio Balancing

The most strategic component involves optimally allocating financial resources across prioritized opportunities through integrated portfolio management techniques rather than standalone budget allotment. Consider budget requests collectively by weighing potential business impact and resource requirements in unison rather than siloed application review. Leadership must guide collaborative trade-off discussions across department leaders to maximize portfolio value holistically. This stage represents the pivot from budget planning to strategy execution.

Step 4: Agile Execution

Finally, retain flexibility to ramp selected initiatives faster or moderate pace where necessary based on field insights, market feedback and milestone assessment. Avoid rigid annual budget commitments without biannual revisits to validate progress and priorities. Nurture a culture that encourages timely requests for funding emerging 'hot spots' by reallocating from 'cooling areas' rather than waiting for next year's cycle.

Activating this playbook positions organizations to benefit from the best of both worlds - stability that incremental budgeting enables and momentum that strategic budgeting catalyzes. Leadership can count on predictable assured spend across core operations funded via traditional budgeting while also fueling ambitious growth programs through dynamic investment pools. Rather than a purely binary choice, integrating both approaches unlocks synergistic value. The creative tension between fostering discipline and pursuing disruption leads to budgeting maturity.

Stitching Together Budgets and Forecasts

Yet no budgeting mechanism can predict market fluctuations perfectly over extended periods. This amplifies the need for budgeting discipline to be complemented by analytical forecasting rigour in navigating business landscape uncertainty. While budgets represent commitment to resourcing priority strategic programs, forecasts serve as sensing mechanisms to understand leading indicators of where markets maybe headed. Any deviations from projected trajectories can then trigger timely budget reprioritizations if necessary.

Forecasting relies on diving into historical performance on key business metrics like sales, revenue, cash flows or even macroeconomic indices to uncover patterns, variations and anomalies. Sophisticated statistical modelling techniques help estimate likely future outcomes based on such trend analyses. But it also requires factoring in potential disruption impacts that past data cannot indicate like changes in competitor dynamics, regulatory reforms, customer sentiment fluctuations or tech innovations.

Simultaneously balancing prudent budgeting with contextual forecasting prevents organizations from either overcommitting resources too early or underpreparing for risks. Alignment between budgets and forecasts also enables seamless adaptation when required. For instance, a sudden demand uptick visible from order forecasts makes it easier for sales leaders to request additional budget for scaling up production capacity swiftly. Equally, leadership finds it simpler to repurpose budgets from initiatives with waning indicator metrics visible through updated forecasts.

Strategic budgeting paired with analytical forecasting provides organizations financial courage and creative confidence to back vision with sustained value creation. No organization today has the luxury of linear operations in markets characterized by exponential disruption. As business environments get increasingly complex, budgets must move beyond accounting tools to become strategy activators. Financial decisions need to stem directly from corporate vision rather than solely factoring historical expenditures. Strategic budgeting serves this imperative by linking resource planning tightly to long-term priority alignment.

Financial Decision-Making Criteria

Whether an individual choosing insurance policies or a business selecting expansion locations, financial decisions permeate our everyday lives. Their implications span from lifestyle comforts to enterprise viability. Consequently, optimizing financial decision-making serves as a pivotal skill for personal progress and organizational success. However, with multifaceted variables at play ranging from risk appetites to ethical dynamics, navigating choices effectively can seem daunting without the right navigational tools. By establishing a structured decision compass to account for key technical and cultural considerations, both individuals and institutions can traverse complexity confidently.

Decision Factors to Consider

Financial literacy fuels effective navigation. Building foundational knowledge on market mechanisms, fiscal policies and portfolio management techniques paves the path for informed choices aligned to objectives. But technical know-how alone provides inadequate direction when pursuing decisions, particularly given dynamic economic conditions. Individual mindsets and organizational values also guide options evaluated and risks perceived, thereby impacting tradeoffs made. Reflecting on preferences and priorities that shape the decision filter beyond technical parameters sets the stage for optimal outcomes.

Specifically, consider four coordinates to plot while charting financial flight plans:

Personal Preferences: Individual personalities, lifestyle goals, values and beliefs drive the strategies deemed appealing, from investment horizons to debt thresholds. Recognizing subjective situational filters builds self-awareness.

Risk Profile: Financial aptitude and risk appetites shape individual decisions, while shareholder expectations and sector dynamics influence business capital allocations. Calibrating risk orientations steers efficient risk-return optimization.

Moral Compass: Ethical standards serve as crucial decision guardrails to balance pursuit of commercial interests with responsible value creation for stakeholders spanning society, environment and future generations.

Market Signals: External dynamics such as competitive shifts, technological disruptions and economic volatility represent uncontrollable yet critical decision inputs framed by limited predictability. Tracking macro forces and indicators sharpens situational analysis.

Internalizing these decision dimensions tackles biases, misconceptions and blind spots to empower objectivity. Just like a GPS leverages latitude, longitude, elevation and terrain to chart efficient routes, factoring these coordinates anchors financial choices to contextual priorities when navigating complexity. But what procedural checkpoints further guide smooth execution?

The Decision Journey

With core decision dimensions providing initial directional grounding, further tailoring a structured procedural flow to evaluate options and select strategies smoothens execution success.

1. Outline specific objectives and desired outcomes targeted to inform screening criteria, be it monthly household budgeting or large-scale mergers. Well-defined intents fuel efficient financial energy expenditure through focused evaluation.

2. Brainstorm alternative routes leveraging multi-disciplinary counsel to maximize choice sets through diversity of thought. Seeking varied perspectives mitigates blind spots and complacency traps arising from historic patterns.

3. Analyze shortlisted options against core decision dimensions outlined earlier - personal preferences, risk considerations, ethical boundaries and external trends. Weighing tradeoffs here sharpens impact projections.

4. Once executing chosen path, continually gauge progress on leading indicators through outcome tracking to enable proactive course co rrections.Financial autopilots fail amidst market turbulence.

Of course tailoring tools like financial planning software, risk analyses and scenario modelling supports technical assessment. But the fluid nature of commercial environments also demands building individual and organizational vigilance muscles. Much like navigational systems, judgements may require periodic reorientations when detours surface. Financial fluency involves mastering this ambidexterity to pair disciplined routines with situational adaptiveness.

Growth often necessitates gradually expanding risk frontiers and decision repertoires. But balancing experimentation with measured reflection is key. In chaotic environments, irrational exuberance warrants tempering just as unreasonable conservatism stifles progress. Leaders need both conviction and flexibility - to commit to strategic intents while also recognizing signals demanding change. This growth mindset with guarded optimism enables navigating financial complexities smoothly.

Rather than chase elusive perfection in decision outcomes, accept tradeoffs as the price for progress in a volatile economic cosmos. Structure processes to filter choices effectively yet retain readiness to occasionally question the premises underlying filtration criteria. Let financial literacy arm you with a multi-dimensional compass but also develop contextual sensitivity to override systemized heuristics when situational wisdom necessitates. By balancing structured protocols with seasoned judgement, individuals and institutions can traverse uncertainty without losing sight of core values and ambition that anchor the true north. Progress then fuels growth without dilution. For through purpose and principle, complexity converts from source of apprehension into opportunity for reward.

Key Takeaways and Final Thoughts on Financial Acumen for Leaders

Key Takeaways:

- Financial literacy serves as an invaluable skill for managerial decision-making and leadership by providing critical context amidst uncertainty. Core concepts like assets, liabilities, financial statements, and metrics form the grammar and vocabulary of this universal language.

- Financial storytelling involves translating raw data into strategic insights by connecting trends to operational priorities. Skilled financial storytelling is crucial for simplifying complexity without losing rigor.

- Building financial fluency relies on mastering fundamentals first through routine immersion, then advancing to contextual analysis before practicing narrative crafting using finances to demonstrate viability.

- Strategic budgeting aligns financial planning with long-term goals by funding key initiatives over incremental percentage lifts. Paired with analytical forecasting, such budgets provide stability and adaptability.

- Structured decision frameworks help evaluate options and tradeoffs based on personal preferences, risk considerations, ethical boundaries and external signals. This multi-dimensional compass anchors choices to contextual priorities.

Mastering the Language of Money

Financial fluency serves as an invaluable yet underappreciated capability for managerial effectiveness and strategic leadership, particularly amidst market uncertainty. By decoding the universal language of money through focused learning rituals, leaders across functions gain an incredible vehicle to guide organizations confidently.

Cultivating financial literacy relies first on demystifying foundational vocabulary and statements to unpack the building blocks. Leaders would do well to routinely review essential documents to then connect observable trends to projects using precise terminology. Such immersion breeds familiarity for numbers to transform from restrictive guidelines to launch pads for opportunity.

Additionally, contextual analysis sharpens the ability to look beyond surface level data to decipher implications and craft narratives. Skilled financial storytelling involves teasing out strategic revelations by simplifying complexity without compromising resolution. It represents translating technical syntax into impactful communication to drive execution.

Finally, ingraining financially informed decision-making habitually prevents overreliance on finance teams for translation. Establishing structured compasses that account for personal preferences, risk considerations, ethical boundaries and external signals anchors tradeoff evaluations and choice optimization.

Financial fluency empowers both individuals and institutions to navigate uncertainty with clearer vision and conviction. By making financial literacy a consistent leadership priority across strategy and operations, organizations can unlock synergies for sustained value creation. The path begins with curiosity to engage numbers instead of avoidance. For through principled and purposeful persistence, the language of money reveals promising pathways forward.

Chapter Eight

Persuasion and Negotiation

Whether convincing employees to adopt innovative processes or persuading executives to fund bold visions, influence and persuasion constitute essential skills for effective leadership. However, the terms are often conflated in everyday discourse. What then differentiates influence from persuasion? Why does mastery of both prove vital for managers driving change? This essay clarifies key distinctions, explores real-world applications and provides tips elevating your abilities engaging others ideas.

Decoding Influence and Persuasion

Influence represents conveying information and framing situations to inspire specific conclusions or actions in groups. For instance, highlighting worrying sales data convinces teams prioritizing customer outreach. Influence establishes logical foundations for ideas through relevant facts and appeals to reason.

Conversely, persuasion denotes directly requesting others adopt beliefs or conduct behaviors aligned to goals. This tends to leverage emotions like inspiration around collective purpose or visions of better futures rather than just rational calculations. Think rallying workers behind ambitious targets through energizing speeches.

Both share a commitment to guide behaviors, not mandate directives. However, influence flows from crafted contexts while persuasion directly asks for commitment. Robert Cialdini, renowned psychologist studying the science of persuasion, notes effective leaders first influence by laying groundwork then persuade by vibrantly envisioning possibilities within those frames.

Applications in Organizations

Understanding differences between influence and persuasion empowers targeting each for distinct organizational challenges:

Influence shines when cold hard data needs unpacking to drive home importance. For example, lukewarm employee engagement survey scores could compel investigating cultural root causes if presented as urgent rather than trivial.

Persuasion matters when connecting teams to corporate values and higher aims. Imagine publicly recognizing volunteers upholding stewardship principles as core to purpose beyond profits.

With complex interdependent systems like enterprises, solely relying on precise quantifications or emotive ambition fuels imbalance. Influence grounds lofty visions in operational realities. Persuasion propels facts into inspired action. One establishes direction, the other momentum.

The Principles of Persuasive Leadership

Persuasion represents an integral capability enabling leaders to influence team alignment around mission-critical goals and inspire peak performance. Rather than coercion, persuasion involves framing priorities and possibilities to compel voluntary engagement. Modern research reveals anyone can strengthen these capacities systematically. These are six science-based techniques elevating persuasiveness in management roles.

Principle 1: Reciprocity

The reciprocity principle denotes that people feel obligated returning favors performed for them. Within a leadership context, managers should offer support, resources or recognition when requesting significant effort towards key objectives so individuals feel valued contributions matter.

For instance, directly praising an employee's unique creativity before requesting they lead ideation for an upcoming brainstorm signal respect while tapping specialized skills needed. Such exchange builds mutual goodwill encouraging cooperation.

Principle 2: Commitment Consistency

Humans tend toward consistent conduct aligning historical commitments once publicly declared or written. Applying this tendency, leaders able to inspire authentic vocalized dedication towards goals wield significant influence ensuring follow-through.

Rather than vaguely expecting accountability, directly yet positively ask staff affirming aligned objectives during meetings. The social pressure and personal reflection cements intentions especially when framed as opportunity rather than obligation. Celebrate commitments to motivate consistency.

Principle 3: Social Proof

Individuals draw consciously and subconsciously from surrounding signals determining appropriate effort and priorities. Visible enthusiasm or apathy proves contagious. Leaders thus maintain responsibility deliberately role modeling desired conduct.

Sharing stories highlighting proactive team members conveys norms of aspiration. Moreover, recognizing contributors publicly for impact beyond expectations fuels intrinsic motivation organizationally. With commitment visible, dedication spreads infectiously between peers.

Principle 4: Authority

Despite valuing autonomy, people often respect expertise viewing industry veterans or management as credible authorities worthy of following. Savvy leaders consequently boost persuasive prowess by showcasing competencies through qualifications, confident decisiveness and developmental investment.

Stay updated reading latest advancements or refining technical skills. Frame suggestions supported by facts and know-how. Earn respect, you gain influence. Authority relies on perceived capability creating competitive advantage.

Principle 5: Liking

Positive personal relationships humanize hierarchies fostering trust and willingness cooperating. Therefore, leaders seeking smooth mobilization around challenging objectives should first cultivate rapport through humble engagement.

Schedule one-on-ones, ask thoughtful questions, actively listen, praise growth and express gratitude. With foundations of mutual understanding built, strategy proposals or ambitious asks won't seem controlling but rather collaborative. Lead through lens of partnership.

Principle 6: Scarcity

People view limited opportunities as inherently more valuable, experiencing fear of missing out elevating urgency. While scarcity principles prove effective short term, overuse risks burnout so leaders must wield judiciously and ethically. Present objectives as time-sensitive and exclusive to decision-makers to accelerate engagement but set reasonable expectations balancing sustainability once enlisted. Prospect of loss summons focus yet everyday realities requiring pacing. Celebrate small milestones to counter drain over months-long campaigns. Strategy sustains motivation more than repeat urgency.

Strategies for Persuasive Leadership

Beyond directive authority, truly visionary leaders inspire teams embracing possibility through artful oratory focused on transformation over coercion. Understanding fundamental rhetorical tactics proves essential cultivating this influential prowess conveying ideas powerfully. Specifically, emphasizing logical appeals, emotional resonance and personal integrity constitutes surefire approach when mobilizing groups towards aspirational horizons.

Establishing Credibility Through Character

Aristotle famously established ethos, or demonstrated strength of character, as foundational for persuasive prowess. When audiences doubt integrity or capability, logical arguments mean little. Leaders must first prove worthy of being followed by showcasing honesty, accountability and dedication to development.

Admit knowledge gaps without hesitation and share personal stories revealing struggle then growth to humanize yourself. Frame life-long learning as imperative, modeling curiosity asking thoughtful questions. With faith in character secured, the vision becomes plausible.

Appealing to Emotions Through Narrative

Pathos, the evocation of resonant sentiment, equally grabs attention while positioning leaders concerned for constituent well-being before personal ego. Savvy storytelling thus represents a seminal skill linking organizational purpose to individual fulfillment.

For example, illustrating how implementing new technology expanded opportunities for a struggling team makes systems upgrades feel mutually beneficial, not just bureaucratic change. Vivid narratives demonstrate you recognize existing pain points through empathetic examples then offer hope tackling challenges aligned to values. By first connecting emotionally, teams open minds to possibilities.

Logically Structuring Requests Around Reality

Finally, logos grounds inspiring visions in operational realities arguing logically why aspirations prove attainable if collective commitment manifests. Leaders must pressure test proposals presenting cogent chains of reasoning addressing implementation barriers then realistically conveying the better future feasible through coordinated effort.

The most ambitious goals remain hallucinations without systematic deconstruction detailing incremental milestone markers leading teams strained but ultimately successful. Share relevant case studies, reference competitors excelling and note when historically similar squads delivered results under your guidance to strengthen credibility around the plausibility path. With logic structuring the approach, groups gain confidence pivoting principles into practice.

Leadership rhetoric balances head and heart, mingling integrity, inspiration and rationality into messages moving people towards transcending limitations. This craft proves perfectible through regular refinement. Listen and align to what truly motivates teams then position your voice championing unified advancement. Through this leadership, transformation unfolds.

The Persuasive Narrative of Stories

Stories speak to hearts in ways sterile data rarely penetrates. Through resonant imagery, emotive dynamics and relatable characterization, stories bind audiences to speakers then compel investment in visions once seeming intangible. Consequently, narrative mastery constitutes seminal skill set separating competent leaders from transformational icons. This piece highlights story craft fundamentals, exemplars and applications elevating persuasive prowess managerially.

Principle 1: Vivid Stories Over Dry Logic

Research affirms that narratives consistently prove more memorable and inciting than enumeration of technical details or statistics alone. Our minds evolved remembering lessons embedded in vivid happenings so well-structured stories tap innate preference for dramatized meaning making.

Leaders should therefore craft narratives featuring suspense, concrete imagery and emotional dynamics that crystallize core messages for recall. Paint pictures with words. Rather than listing accomplishments show how success manifested through described experience. Allow the story do rhetorical heavy lifting.

Principle 2: Relatable Characters Over Abstract Actors

Similarly, identifiable personalities rendered richly through hopes, struggles and growth arcs elicit listener investment exponentially more than vague generalizations regarding anonymous actors. Persuasion flows from eliciting empathy then offering cathartic breakthroughs.

Therefore, carefully characterize protagonists that the target audience relates to then position your vision as instrumental overcoming described challenges. Employees connect with rookie managers nervously seeking commanding respect through displays of confidence and commitment staying true to self. We invest in heroic becoming.

Principle 3: Clear Lessons Over Subtle Implications

Finally, persuasive stories crystallize rather than camouflage core morals to ensure clarity of takeaways. Without explicitly naming key insights from the narrative, listeners often derive idiosyncratic inferences missing speaker intent entirely. Guide understanding by concise reflection on pivotal moments before tying directly to strategic ends requiring buy-in.

For example, recall that scene featuring determination despite setbacks then emphasize how the same perseverance now drives proposed growth initiatives dependent on united persistence. Script dramatic moments then clearly connect dots to desired adoption. Bold visions manifest when groups share lessons learned from legacies.

Legendary Tech Visionary

The late Steve Jobs exemplified harnessing personal narratives to compellingly convey ambitious visions. During Apple's ascension, Jobs famously framed product launches through engaging stories positioning offerings as revolutionary vehicles for human empowerment beyond utility.

By interweaving accounts of his unconventional explorations in calligraphy, meditation, and design appreciation, Jobs illustrated the creative synthesis underpinning Apple's innovation then invited listeners recognizing similar inner yearning for tools unleashing their untapped gifts. Instead of enumerated specs, he offered stories of purpose then belonging. We purchased products embodying shared transcendence from convention, not just sleek devices. Masterful persuaders enroll hearts before minds.

Influential Movement Builder

Likewise, Facebook's Sheryl Sandberg leverages blend of demographic data and vulnerable self-disclosure spotlighting gender inequality in corporate leadership then advocating systemic changes.

Combining authoritative statistics with personal stories of exclusion and lessons learned, Sandberg makes abstract policy problems deeply felt through narrative. We understand challenges facing talented women through depicted experience then acknowledge complicity in outdated cultural norms. Once accepted, solution pathways feel obvious extending equal opportunities advancing collective capability. Sandberg first connects woman to woman before partnering allies in power.

At core, stories build cooperation converting strangers into protagonists jointly invested sharing future outcome. Wield narrative as scalable leadership strategy.

Negotiation Strategies

Negotiation represents an indispensable capacity enabling leaders to reconcile divergent perspectives, mediate conflicts, and foster mutually-beneficial relationships furthering organizational interests. However, with limited frameworks guiding skill development, many managers approach critical conversations armed only with intuitive instincts. This comprehensive guide outlines research-backed techniques for elevating your negotiation abilities to drive win-win growth agreements. Let's examine core principles, emotional intelligence factors, and communication tactics distinguishing truly masterful negotiators.

Seeking Mutual Victory

The essence of principled negotiation entails identifying shared interests allowing both parties targeting acceptable outcomes given situational constraints. Rather than zero-sum mentalities where limited resources mean contested compromise, adept negotiators expand inventive possibilities satisfying stakeholders jointly.

For example, union leaders appealing to corporate values around safety and stewardship when bargaining for workplace improvements frames change as an investment uplifting morale and productivity simultaneously rather than just hiking labor costs. Find shared purpose in advance.

Let Counterparties Anchor Offers

Additionally, allowing counterparts to open negotiations by presenting initial offers showcases constraints informing our responsive targets untethered from assumption. If marketing promises deliverable campaign conversions 30% above actuals, we anchor plans in realities not baseless optimism when making budgeting counter-offers.

Patient responsive listening exposes true capabilities, resources available or needs required for shared success more accurately than asserting potentially unrealistic demands we then anchor to despite disconfirming data. Lead from behind in negotiation.

Self & Social Awareness

Renowned Yale management professor Jeff Thompson declares "emotional and social intelligence separate great negotiators from average ones." Those laser focused on immediate technical details prove unable adapting direction fluidly based on counterpart reactions. Masterful relationship leaders listen, understand emotional landscapes then redirect accordingly.

For example, recognizing frustrated body language coupled with avoidance of eye contact signals unspoken anxieties troublesome if ignored. Adaptively empathizing though builds connections vital for exchanges of authentic needs and creative problem solving. Sharp social perception proves foundational.

Self & Impulse Regulation

But perceptiveness alone fails creating workable alignments without self-regulation managing internal reactions first. Reactive expressions of anger, hurt or fear undermine rational progress by signaling untrustworthiness intensifying tensions. Restraint allows constructive priorities surfacing.

Leaders must therefore govern impulsive responses through tactics like mindfulness, cognitive reappraisal of benign interpretations for negative behaviors and forgiving past counterparty mistakes. With reflective space opened, negotiated logic leads. Suppress reactivity in favor of positivity.

Establish Rapport via Personal Sharing

Beyond governing reactions, proactive displays of understanding also dismantle relational barriers to cooperation. When negotiating intensely personal issues, tactical vulnerability through transparency around aligned experiences builds crucial social capital and rapport.

For example, during tense coaching conversations with struggling staff, managers noting parallel prior development hardships makes path forward appear supportive not persecutory. We connect compassions before correcting course. Diplomacy develops through humility.

Listen Actively to Learn Interests

Rather than passively hearing words, active listening unpacks meanings and intent through engaged inquiry. What issues seem nonnegotiable? Which terms reflect must-haves versus nice-to-haves? When did described tensions start escalating? Mining beneath positions unearths motivations informing them.

Insight into stakeholder mindsets, pressures and priorities guides tailoring proposals maximizing mutual return. Without grasping where people stand benefits wise, progress stalls. Thus leaders listen first, then lead second.

Ask Empowering Questions

Finally, siphon insights using empathetic questioning focused on resolution not antagonism. "How can we nurture trust moving forward here?" beats combative interrogations attacking integrity like "How could you make that reckless decision?!"

Frame queries assuming positive intent, then invite brainstorming solutions integrating both perspectives. Presume partners equally want organizational advancement but hold unique positions limiting purview. Seek shared truth.

Negotiative excellence springs from emotional and social intelligence coupled with acumen generating win-win proposals through integrative communication. Lead by listening then leverage learning to advance collectively.

Key Takeaways and Final Thoughts on Persuasion and Negotiation

Key Takeaways:

- Influence involves framing situations using logic and facts to inspire conclusions while persuasion makes direct emotional appeals asking for commitment. Leaders optimize outcomes combining approaches.

- Six principles constitute universal techniques for persuasive leadership: reciprocity, consistency, social proof, authority, liking and scarcity. Apply contextually.

- Storytelling represents a seminal persuasive skillset. Craft compelling narratives featuring suspense, vivid imagery and relatable characters that illuminate lessons.

- Negotiation excellence relies on emotional intelligence, impulse control and asking empowering questions focused on reconciling interests, not attacking positions. Identify shared purpose.

The Leader's Scaling Advantage: Persuasion, Negotiation and Collective Achievement

Interpersonal abilities distinguishing influential leaders from average managers depend enormously on persuasion and negotiation acumen. Through masterful communication aligning groups behind inspired vision, seemingly impossible objectives become manifest able. Teams transcend individual limitations expanding potential exponentially when united by narrative and guided through impediments by nimble diplomacy.

Yet rhetorical skills prove perfectible through practice and coaching. Distinctions separating strong from weak negotiators trace to learned behaviors, not innate charisma. Thus by investing in emotional intelligence, persuasive storytelling and needs-focused conflict resolution, leaders gain access to virtuous cycles securing compounding returns over tenure.

Chapter Nine

Strategic Reorganization

Leaders face the constant challenge of ensuring their organizations remain aligned, engaged, and empowered in service of strategic goals. However, even the most thoughtfully designed structures and processes can become misaligned over time as internal and external conditions evolve. Savvy leaders recognize reorganization as a pivotal opportunity requiring as much finesse as forethought. Rather than seeking structural perfection, strategic leaders artfully realign people, power, and priorities to drive enduring transformation.

When approached strategically, reorganization achieves three key leadership outcomes:

1. Structural realignment

2. Power rebalancing

3. Expectations resetting across all levels of an organization

Thoughtful structure realignment responds to changing needs and conditions to keep organizational frameworks relevant. As market landscapes, customer expectations, technologies, and even corporate strategies shift over time, what once operated smoothly may become cumbersome or counterproductive. astute leaders recognize the need for structural realignment, whether refining departmental configurations, reporting lines, decision-making pathways, or process flows. While structure plays a key role, it is rarely the sole driver of reorganization.

Behind most structural realignments lies a parallel opportunity: rebalancing power. Seasoned leaders understand organizational power comes not only from formal positional authority, but also from informal networks, subject matter mastery, and accumulated goodwill. Long-standing power barons often accumulate influence rivaling even the titular organizational monarch. Rather than attacking barons directly, politically savvy kings and queens cleverly redistribute authority and decision-making to create balanced organizational power. With former spheres of control disrupted and key supporters repositioned, even longtime barons again show proper fealty to the throne. Through graceful rather than brash power balancing, thoughtful leaders avoid uncontrolled turmoil.

Finally, reorganization offers leaders a chance to reset expectations organization-wide. This two-way communication process clarifies leadership priorities as well as desired employee mindsets and working styles. Many expectations reflect long-held organizational assumptions and norms, remaining unspoken yet understood by veteran employees and cultural insiders. Bringing these tacit expectations to the surface gives leaders an opportunity to formally reinforce or redirect norms in alignment with present-day needs. Additionally, resetting expectations gives individual contributors a chance to clarify what they need from leadership to excel in new initiatives or structures. By proactively realigning expectations around behaviors, communication, collaboration, autonomy, innovation, leadership access, development opportunities, and more, strategic leaders invest employees at all levels in shared future success.

Traditional logic advocates designing ideal organizational structures to support current corporate strategy. Such clinical, consultant-friendly advice ignores on-the-ground realities facing actual leaders. In practice, today's most effective leaders take a nuanced view of reorganization. Rather than theoretical perfection, they cleverly reshape existing human capabilities to drive strategy execution and growth. Though structure remains relevant, truly strategic leaders look first to talent, politics, and culture when reorganizing. Leveraging reorganization's unique power to redirect people, influence, priorities and norms, masterful leaders realign their organizations to maintain relevance and sustain competitive dominance over time. With equal parts insight, influence, and incisiveness, leaders turn reorganization's upheaval into enduring strategic gain.

Acting Decisively to Refocus your Team

Leaders know one key to driving enduring success is assembling a leadership squad fully empowered and aligned to achieve strategic goals. However, even well-designed teams and structures require realignment over time as conditions and priorities shift. When reorganization comes due, decisive leaders act quickly to resolve uncertainty, redirect focus, and reengage talent.

The ideal time for leaders to reorganize is early in their tenure. Within initial months, newly appointed leaders restructure to implement needed changes decisively. Resist holding back to further analyze or gradually tweak teams. Act boldly instead to rapidly revamp the team and remove doubt.

Decisive reorganization achieves three vital outcomes: installing the right leadership, minimizing uncertainty, and signaling fresh expectations. First, act quickly to implement your leadership vision and approach. Surround yourself with the mix of capabilities and chemistry needed to drive performance. Carrying forward misaligned leaders slows momentum, strains culture, and shows indecision.

Second, rapid revamping removes organizational uncertainty that breeds politicking and erodes morale over time. The longer leaders wait to restructure, the more anxiety spreads. Nip fear and doubt in the bud by acting definitively early on. Avoid analysis paralysis or slow tweaks that suggest incremental rather than wholesale shifts.

Finally, rapid reorganization signals change is here to stay, old ways no longer apply, and fresh expectations take hold. When leaders act boldly, they put everyone on notice—the path forward mandates new mindsets and capabilities. Gradual change implies the old DNA still holds sway.

Decisive reorganization requires leaders first and foremost to act swiftly when transitioning people out of roles. Lingering "lame duck" leaders strain teams and puncture confidence. Once tough "kill the king" decisions are made, move people out rapidly while supporting their dignity and providing next-step counsel.

With staffing changes resolved, redirect everyone's focus forward to business growth and results. Assure remaining talent they are valued contributors to future success. With the reorganization dust settled, leaders must reengage teams around refreshed vision and priorities with clarity, consistency, and conviction.

Reorganization is a pivotal moment to reset team engagement and alignment. Executed decisively, a bold restructuring lays the foundation for future success. Leaders who act rapidly and resolutely to implement changes send a definitive signal: the future will not resemble the past. A brisk, transparent reorganization sets the stage for achieving strategic goals through focused execution.

Leading Organizational Change

Leading successful change remains essential, yet ever-more complex, for today's leaders. With uncertainty and transformation now constants, organizational change leadership has become a daily requirement rather than an occasional event. Unfortunately, historical data shows most major change initiatives fail outright. In navigating relentless change, leaders thus require both understanding of key change leadership concepts and nimble, customizable approaches.

At its core, organizational change involves fundamentally upgrading one or more foundational component, like culture, systems, or workflow. Rather than tweaking isolated processes, major change strikes at the organizational heart. Leaders must guide stakeholders in reinventing underlying assumptions, behaviors, and structures to meet emerging challenges and opportunities.

Change arises from two root causes: repairing broken elements or pursuing strategic improvements. The former often sparks from gradual declines in organizational health and performance. Think neglected upkeep and efficiency losses over time, or cultural disconnects around values or diversity. Here change equates to essential, if painful, catch-up to reclaim lost capability.

The second driver, opportunity-led change, stems from leaders' ambition, not organizational crisis. Major innovations, new strategies, and evolving customer expectations prompt proactive, offensive organizational change. Think redefining industries, not just playing catch-up.

In both cases, leaders must understand change exists on a spectrum spanning adaptive to transformational. Adaptive changes incrementally enhance existing approaches through gradual, iterative improvement. Leadership here involves encouraging ongoing learning and tweaks within current frameworks.

Transformational change violently upends the status quo as radical new structures, systems, and processes emerge. Leadership focuses on communicating a compelling vision while managing the human struggle inherent to dramatic change. Stakeholder mindsets and capabilities require wholesale shift.

The complexity leaders face is that much organizational change lives between purely adaptive and wholly transformational. Elements of both incremental and dramatic change intermix. This demands leaders accurately diagnose change drivers and magnitudes at play across the organizational ecosystem. With context clarified, they can then skillfully apply appropriate change leadership approaches - balancing impatient ambition with empathy, transparency with decisiveness. Successfully navigating change obliges leaders to embrace this inherent dynamism.

How to Lead a Reorganization

Leading successful large-scale change remains one of today's most complex yet critical leadership skills. With business volatility the norm, organizations must continually adapt or risk extinction. However, the harsh reality is that most major change initiatives fail outright - stalled by inertia, skepticism, or poor execution. In navigating relentlessuncertainty, leaders require both a strong grasp of research-backed change methodologies as well as the flexibility to customize approaches. By artfully blending change science and situation-specific adaptability, today's most effective leaders guide stakeholders to embrace and thrive amidst transformation.

The Organizational Change Process

Organizational change spans both structural and cultural components, obliging leaders to rethink underlying assumptions, behaviors, systems, and processes. Rather than isolated process tweaks, major change strikes at entrenched traditions and workflows. To systematically implement high-magnitude changes, Harvard research offers the aptly named CHANGE model encompassing six key steps:

1. *Conceptualize* – Leaders first seek root cause clarity into exactly what is driving the need for change, including external and internal factors at play. Resist jumping to conclusions or solutions. Thoroughly investigate subtle yet critical nuances across culture, strategy, structure, operations, and technology to pinpoint true change catalysts.

2. *Hear* – Next, gather input from diverse stakeholders at all levels to illuminate additional factors leaders may overlook. The goal here is to exhaustively gather richest-possible data and perspectives on the change drivers, challenges, and impacts at hand.

3. *Agenda* – With robust understanding established, shift to setting the actual change agenda and priorities. Define specific elements requiring upgrade or transformation to address root causes. Shape a compelling vision for change and clarify near and longer-term goals.

4. *Nexus* – Identify the specific parts of the organizational ecosystem – structure, workflow, culture, skills, etc. – needing redesign to enable the change agenda. Determine the optimal sequencing and interdependencies across targeted changes.

5. *Guide and Govern* – Focus shifts to active leadership communication, modeling desired mindsets and behaviors, maintaining alignment via feedback channels, and course-correcting based on progress and responses.

6. *Engage and Execute* – Leaders and managers cascade clarified expectations, development support, and visible modeling/reinforcement to encourage stakeholder adoption. Meanwhile, execution continues iteratively against the change plan.

In examining the model's steps, leaders should view the first three as analytical input gathering and planning. The latter three represent active leadership communication, support, and accountability to drive adoption. Yet unlike rigid stage-gate processes, the model should be applied iteratively and situationally versus in strict order.

Gaining Insight: Conceptualize and Hear

Early phases center on deeply comprehending exactly what change aims to achieve within the organizational ecosystem. Leaders avoid assumptions or preconceived notions by thoroughly investigating subtle cultural nuances, power dynamics, skills gaps, and incentive structures to pinpoint root causes. Key insights often emerge through respectful stakeholder inquiry spanning formal leaders to frontline teams. The goal of exhaustive upfront inquiry is precisely defining the issues requiring intervention before designing solutions.

Building Conviction: Agenda and Nexus

With robust clarity into change drivers, leaders shift to defining the agenda for actual transformation. This demands focus and courage to identify sacred cows requiring slaughter, even amidst skepticism or discomfort. Leaders must paint a compelling vision of a future state that persuasively rationalizes disruption. Defining implementation nexuses involves pinpointing the specific culture shifts, process changes, skill building, and structural realignments essential to fulfilling the agenda. Prioritization and sequencing should balance material outcomes with confidence-building wins.

Activation and Adoption: Guide, Govern, Engage and Execute

With planning solidified, leaders switch gears to active change leadership communication and support. Now the priority becomes influencing mindsets and behaviors across management layers. Gaining adoption requires persistent, multi-channel communication of not just what is changing, but why alignment matters. Meanwhile, leaders and managers must champion the vision while addressing real human concerns. Finally, the change plan rolls out iteratively, enabled by capability building, feedback channels, and course corrections.

While detailed structure helps guide disciplined thinking, effective change leadership also obliges reading culture, making situational judgment calls, and customizing approaches accordingly. Leaders artfully blend change science with empathy, communication savvy, and contextual wisdom. By doing so, they can convert even dramatic disruption into energizing progress against shared strategic goals. Ultimately, skilful change leadership weaves systematic process with the human realities of fear, doubt, and desire for purpose. Savvy leaders illuminate the path ahead while making each stakeholder feel essential to getting there.

Communicating to Inspire and Overcoming Resistance

Leading successful transformational change obliges today's leaders to artfully blend systematic planning with nuanced soft skills essential to winning hearts and minds. Beyond technical expertise, change leadership demands clearly communicating an inspiring vision while empathetically addressing inherent human concerns. Research confirms that without persuasive messaging and active resistance management fully half of all major change efforts fail outright. By investing equal energy in both inspiration and adoption, leaders can beat the odds to lead stakeholders through productive disruption.

Crafting a Compelling Change Vision

The vision lies at the heart of leading change. Through vision, leaders paint a vivid picture of a boldly different future state, one requiring stakeholders to advance both individually and collectively. The vision sets the destination, rationalizes the journey, and motivates action even amidst discomfort.

Yet many leaders fall short not due to lack of imagination, but ineffective communication. Common pitfalls include defaulting to amorphous jargon that obscures meaning and failing to address intrinsic human questions of "What's in it for me?" and "How, exactly, will this work?" Leaders undermine vision traction by solely broadcasting high-level messages absent connective, tailored communication.

Research suggests four crucial elements of resonating vision communication during change:

Clarity - Avoid empty buzzwords and management speak through illustrative metaphor, story, or visuals conveying tangible meaning. Help individuals see how their roles concretely change.

Specificity - While vision sets direction, people need granularity to appropriately modify behaviors and systems. Detail how workflow, decision authority, and collaboration will differ going forward.

Relevance - Connect the vision and people's contributions to shared mission and values. This intrinsic purpose, not just incentives, stimulates engagement amid difficulty.

Continuity - Affirm elements of culture and strengths that will persist despite changes. People interpret new ideas through the lens of the familiar - leverage this.

By investing in multi-channel clarity, relevance, specificity, and continuity, leaders turn communication into inspiration. Vision brings change to life by spotlighting how and why. When elevated through care and creativity, vision communication fuels stakeholders past uncertainty toward collective ambition.

Managing Inevitable Resistance

While compelling vision eases the path, leaders still encounter resistance given change's disruptive nature. Left unaddressed, resistance manifests through disengagement, excuses, work declines, sabotage, or outright rebellion. Managing resistance represents change leaders' second pivotal task.

Resistance inevitably arises from both rational objections and psychological self-preservation. Change obliges uncomfortable cognitive and behavioral shifts while surfacing job impacts, shifted power dynamics, and uncertainty. Leaders err when simplistically dismissing resistance as ignorance or malice rather than thoughtfully addressing underlying issues.

Resistance drivers include:

- Personal impacts - Will I have the requisite skills, authority, resources? What work changes lie ahead?

- Credibility concerns - Do I trust leadership's motives and competence to lead this change?

- Values misalignment - Does this change conflict with what I believe is right?

- Past failures - Have prior changes succeeded or just caused headaches?

- Life disruption - How will this affect my work-life balance and stability?

While resistance manifests individually, it generally clusters around several key behaviors including:

- Emotional responses - anxiety, anger, sadness, avoidance

- Passive defiance - disengagement, excuses, silos, workflow drags

- Active pushback - arguments, gossip, idea sabotage

- Overcorrection - aggression, micro-management, control needs

With clarity into common resistance drivers and behaviors, leaders can plan targeted preemption and response. A core tenet of resistance management obliges leaders across the hierarchy to promptly, directly address resistance through courageous yet compassionate dialogue. Leaders demonstrate willingness to adapt while affirming that change is essential and inevitable.

Beyond courage, leaders require practical frameworks to guide resistance management. Prosci research offers two key avenues:

1. Resistance Prevention - Proactively anticipate and mitigate resistance through early, transparent communication, capability-building, and culture reinforcement.

2. Resistance Response - Once resistance endures, thoughtfully diagnose root issues and respond with appropriate corrective actions - be they more change resources or consequences.

Within this framework, leaders play orchestrators while managers become "resistance first responders". Line leaders maintain direct visibility into emerging behaviors and issues ripe for early intervention. Equipped by executive leadership with robust messaging and tools, managers surface concerns, redirect outliers, affirm strengths, and adapt support. This distributed mitigation model counters resistance gaining momentum across silos and sites.

While slick vision and incentives drive willing adopters, resistance management secures the middle majority. Leaders signal through early resistance wins that objection is allowable yet obstruction unacceptable. Over time, initial resentment gives way to acknowledged benefits of progress. In lockstep with inspiration, artful resistance leadership turns adversity into energy behind shared ambition.

Talent Retention Strategies During Reorganization

Leaders understand that organizational change obliges rethinking nearly everything: vision, structure, workflow, culture, and capability mix. Yet in this tumult the single most pivotal asset remains motivated talent. Skilled people ultimately conceive strategy, build solutions, win customers, and evolve culture. Disruptive times heighten the risks of losing irreplaceable institutional knowledge, relationships, and future leadership. By artfully retaining pivotal talent during change leaders secure the engine enabling transformation and continuity amid volatility.

Common but Flawed Approaches

Conventional wisdom preaches using incentives to retain talent during turbulent transitions like reorganizations or mergers. Throw more compensation at critical contributors to keep them settled, focused, and loyal. Intuitively this makes sense and sometimes works sufficiently. However, research and experience show heavy reliance on financial retention tactics as suboptimal for several reasons:

Incentives alone rarely persuade - at-risk talent consider many complex factors beyond immediate income. Pay assuages some uncertainty but does not address underlying identity, purpose, and capability concerns permeating change.

Scattering incentives too widely squanders resources while protecting many already loyal. Precision targeting of swing groups proves far more economical and effective.

Leaders risk commoditizing talent relationships into simplistic transactional exchanges. However, inspiring service-oriented cultures centers on intrinsic purpose and belonging, not bonuses.

Sharper Approaches - Targeted, Multimodal Retention

Superior retention strategies oblige leaders first thoroughly identifying at-risk talent segments, then deploying customized value exchanges addressing both rational and emotional considerations. Retention derives from resonance.

More rigorous talent segmentation spotlights swing groups; those at higher risk of voluntarily exiting during change yet also essential to continuity or transformation. Common defining criteria include:

- *Strategic impact* - What talent loss most threatens change success or business continuity?

- *Transferability* - Which skills and relationships are hardest to replace?

- *Flight risk* - Who shows early disengagement signaling departure potential?

Thoughtful segmentation reveals pivotal subsets beyond typical high-potentials. Leaders uncover "hidden gems"; experienced managers or subject experts well down formal hierarchies yet central to daily operations or change execution. Their sheer invisibility to senior leaders heightens impulse to exit.

Likewise, leaders assess variance in mindsets across swing groups to discern rational and emotional hot buttons. Research suggests two archetypes commonly emerge:

- *Change resisters* - Those wary of personal or family disruption from relocations, shifts in authority, or job impacts from reorganization. Loss of stability and identity loom large.

- *Opportunity seekers* - Talent ambivalent about change yet alert for better options internally or externally. They prioritize career growth and leadership development over stability.

Of course myriad blends of sentiment exist, but parsing differences enables customized value exchanges. Note financial packages alone satisfy neither main archetype; intrinsic incentives matter equally here.

With crisp talent segments and sentiments mapped, leaders lastly define retention strategies addressing both rational and emotional dynamics within each group. Tactics balance non-financial value exchanges and financial incentives structured to signal future opportunity.

Securing Your Change Resisters

For talent uneasy about change disruption, emphasize continuity, support, and stability. Retention for this group centers on defusing transition adversity to maintain lives and productivity without existential anxiety. Core tactics include:

- *Family/lifestyle support* - Fund key needs like household relocation, childcare, or career coaching for significant others impacted by moves or schedule changes.

- *Flexible work options* - Reassure by providing partial remote work, flexible scheduling, or other unique arrangements easing personal disruption.

- *Outplacement services* - Some situations may warrant supporting external transitions gracefully for all parties. Transparency and dignity count.

- *Cross-training* - Ensure critical institutional knowledge gets passed on, demonstrating respect while reducing induced anxiety from feeling irreplaceable.

- *Transition coaching* - Provide mentors or sounding boards to validate concerns and discuss navigation strategies during rollercoaster change cycles.

- *Stay incentives* - Balance the above intrinsic support with modest financial incentives for staying the course. Cash helps but doesn't compel.

Incentivizing Your Opportunity Seekers

For talent viewing impending change as a catalyst to advance their career internally or expand horizons externally, the focus shifts from security to growth. Retention for this group means spotlighting exciting new leadership challenges and development pathways. Core tactics include:

- High-visibility assignments - Attach emerging leaders to key initiatives central to the change agenda. Let them put their stamp on something important while working with senior executives.

- Accelerated promotions - Elevate top talent into enlarged roles with more authority, scope, and team leadership much faster than during stable periods.

- Mentor access - Ensure next-generation leaders receive 1:1 mentorship from senior leaders invested in their perspective and trajectory. Avoid lost voices.

- Funded education - Support continuous learning cycles including external certifications, conferences, and degree programs aligned to change plans and higher-level advancement.

- Stretch bonuses - Incentivize top performance on key assignments essential to change outcomes via bonuses paid over time. Allows higher comp aligned to priority initiatives.

The aim for both sets of tactics seeks to align individual and organizational interests through supportive, aspirational value exchanges versus rigid transactional ones. People give their best amid adversity when treated as partners behind a shared mission - not just contractual labor bought with minimal, temporary incentives.

Essential Change Leadership Enablers

While specialized retention tactics help preserve pivotal talent, leaders cannot outsource engagement solely to programs during turbulence. Successful retention derives directly from day-to-day organizational culture and behaviors modeled by leaders throughout change journeys.

Trust and transparency set the stage. Leaders who actively communicate "why" behind change, involve teams in "how" execution choices, and admit uncertainty balance conviction with compassion. They address tough issues directly while responding to input. People cope with even disruptive change provided the rationale resonates with mission and the pace suits context.

Likewise, leaders staying visible and accessible ease uncertainty. They celebrate contributions, explain pending shifts, actively listen to concerns, and credit teams publicly. During major transitions, the intrinsic incentives of purpose, connection, appreciation, and future opportunity retain talent that money alone cannot.

Finally, leaders invest themselves through times of volatility. They redefine visions, reallocate resources, rethink structures, but also refuge and reenergize talent. Leaders model resilience alongside vulnerability by sharing their own discomfort. But they also spotlight how talent powers the collective path forward.

In organizational change, retaining pivotal people ultimately retains competitive advantage. Talent retains best when aligned to mission, equipped for shared success, and appreciated as partners beyond the turbulence. Savvy leaders realize no formulaic incentives program replaces the personal, authentic engagement obligatory to inspire talent to stay the course. Teams give their all when treated as such rather than temporary assets to be periodically recalibrated and retained using short-term financial enticements. For forward-looking leaders, real retention flows from lived culture and values, not compensation.

Key Takeaways and Final Thoughts on Strategic Reorganization

Key Takeaways:

- Executing reorganization successfully requires clearly communicating the rationale while also addressing people's intrinsic uncertainty and concerns. Leaders must both inspire hearts and assuage fears.

- Speed and decisiveness in announcing and implementing structural changes is essential. This promptly reduces organizational anxiety so focus can shift to strategic execution.

- Major organizational change obliges artfully balancing systematic project rigor with soft skills to persuade, motivate, and support teams. Structure enables, culture embodies.

- Vision provides the crucial focal point guiding productive transformation. Leaders must paint a vivid, relatable picture of the future state and why it compels bold moves.

- Resistance is inevitable given disruption inherent in reorganization. Leaders should plan proactive resistance management frameworks focused on early stage intervention.

- Retaining pivotal talent throughout volatility is central to continuity and minimizing loss of institutional knowledge. Customized value exchanges addressing both rational and emotional considerations retain best.

Leading Disruptive Change Through Supportive Continuity

In times of organizational change, leaders face an apparent paradox - thoughtfully disrupting embedded structures and processes while providing continuity, confidence and support enabling talent to thrive in new systems. Yet leaders who embrace this nuance as creative tension unlock lasting value. By artfully reorganizing to simultaneously refocus vision and reenergize teams, they pave the way for strategic renewal, improved performance, and sustained competitive dominance.

The need for organizational change is frequent yet the undertaking full of hazard. Leaders must dismantle legacy systems and realign talent while avoiding talent exodus or operational meltdowns. Reorganization obliges both creating an inspiring vision for the future and supporting people through the present ambiguity. At its core, leading strategic reorganization requires communicating to inspire hearts while managing resistance.

Vision provides a crucial focal point amid swirling uncertainty. Through vivid language and metaphor, leaders spotlight how pending changes support the core mission and values already resonating with talent. Vision provides continuity of purpose enabling discontinuous near-term disruption. Likewise, decisively finalizing structural changes rapidly reduces uncertainty so focus can shift from anxiety to priorities.

Of course inspiration alone is insufficient given inherent people disruption during reorganization. Deliberate support and change management frameworks ease the transition by addressing well-founded human concerns about new roles, responsibilities, skills needs, and potential volatility. Leaders signal through organizational actions at each step that talent remains the priority now and for the future.

The apparent paradox of disruptive change and supportive continuity dissolves when leaders guide with courage and compassion. Structures continuously evolve, but mission and talent empowering the mission endure. By artfully reorganizing to simultaneously refocus and reenergize, leaders transform identity without losing essence. The result - strategic renewal unfolding with talent along for an essential journey, not left in the wake.

Chapter Ten

Conclusion

Across preceding chapters, we traversed the landscape distinguishing strategic leaders - those rare visionaries translating ambitious dreams into collective reality amidst complexity. By spotlighting crucial cognitive capacities, interpersonal abilities, and executional structures, this playbook equipped readers for elevating leadership impact dramatically.

Now at journey's end, we revisit touchstone takeaways while contextualizing principles within larger themes of thriving amidst uncertainty. For leading strategically necessitates both firm roots anchoring efforts against distraction and flexible stems capitalizing on emergent opportunities. Progress relies on reconciling this inherent tension creatively.

We opened by homing vital metaskills for simplifying complexity without over-simplifying reality. Constructing situational mental models through techniques brings clarity amidst noise. Then regulation of anxiety and impatience unlocks sound judgement under duress when stakes intensify. Leaders additionally cultivate foresight by envisioning multiple futures, both best case turnarounds and worst case contingencies. Thereby they mentally rehearse responses preparing for turbulence. With such cognitive capacities, volatility holds less disruptive sway.

We next focused on committing to strategic priorities after informed sense-making. Discovery-driven planning shifts traditional models by starting with open questions instead of prepackaged solutions given continuous contextual change. Then establishing line of sight between vision, departmental key performance indicators and individual goals sustains alignment on what matters most. Additionally, financial fluency serves as an underappreciated vehicle for strategic communication clarifying market factors and resource tradeoffs while persuading stakeholders.

With direction set, execution relies on influence and accountability. We covered an array of persuasion techniques informed by reciprocity, consistency, and storytelling craft for inspiration. Additionally, conflict resolution through non-positional negotiation expands possibility by identifying mutually beneficial trades reconciling interests. With vision resonating through hearts and minds, the stage is set for aligned achievement.

Our final section addressed embedding adaptable rhythms across projects, performance management and continuous improvement programs. Governed agile execution contains risk while accelerating learnings to inform strategy evolution. Cascading OKRs measurement frequently but also dedicated analysis time to make systemic improvements keeps progress unfolding. Ultimately constructing deliberate developmental loops organization-wide sustains optimization.

Steering progress amidst perpetual uncertainty requires grounding in timeless principles yet responsiveness to emerging conditions. And while disambiguating complexity relies on rational skillsets, actualizing strategy necessitates emotional resonance across stakeholders. Therefore, strategic leadership obliges artful balance of inspiration and organization. Shared values anchor collective efforts yet adaptable systems propel initiatives forward fluidly.

By embracing this paradox, leaders transform disruption from debilitating distraction into springboards for innovation. They view change as the only constant, progress as perpetual refinement and setbacks as feedback furthering understanding. Thereby possibilities stay abundantly clear despite ambiguity in the path ahead. Conviction for the future sustains consistent momentum even when specific tactics require calibration to evolving realities.

Of course organizations cannot respond nimbly at scale without localized empowerment across business units closer to ground-level trends. Strategic leaders thereby pivot from directive authority figures towards facilitators of aligned contribution guided by common purpose. They delegate decisions whenever reasonable while concentrating executive efforts on priority setting and capability building. Trust in human potential seeds growth mindsets unlocking latent talent.

Yet granting autonomy requires responsibility in exchange. Broad stakeholder participation only enhances outcomes if efforts remain professionally accountable to results and relational considerations. Therefore, leaders establish psychologically safe environments for candid dialogue while upholding high standards for excellence. By balancing empowerment with expectations, strategic leaders realize exponentially greater collective achievement.

Despite dizzying uncertainty ahead, possibility persists for leaders committed to lifelong learning and uplifting others. While technical skills demand consistent renewal amidst exponentially advancing workplace technology, timeless human principles maintain relevance. Curiosity, empathy and courage hold strong whatever coming decades herald.

Strategic leaders embodying such virtues will continue transcending perceived constraints by artfully inspiring hearts, aligning priorities and structuring dynamic execution engines. They realize that sustainable solutions to multidimensional challenges require diverse thinkers united by shared purpose. And they understand that realizing ambitious visions relies on decentralized contribution rather than unilateral heroics alone.

This book sought to equip readers for leading amid complexity by spotlighting research-backed insights paired with relatable demonstrative stories. Building strategic leadership capabilities requires commitment to continuous upgrading given inevitable environmental change. But you, the reader, stand well-prepared for the journey having learned how to learn.

Now at the frontier between current reality and latent potential, a seminal question looms - where will you guide your organization next in pursuit of positive impact? How quickly and capably can your team execute today's plan while retaining readiness to responsively adapt?

With an empowered squad aligned to vision and adaptive execution engines primed for fluid course correction, realize that progress has no ceiling. Therefore choose goals advancing frontiers of human dignity, sustainable prosperity and inclusive justice without self-imposed limits. For there exists no constraint beyond the reach of leaders mastering strategy while uplifting others. Now boldly embark with your crew towards horizons bright.